God Incidents

Real-Life Stories to Strengthen and Restore Your Faith

Rev. Dr. Glenn M. Wagner

Ava & Rex,

You are a blessing.

[signature]

EBook MyBook L.L.C.

For more information and further discussion, visit
glennmwagner.com

Published by Ebook MyBook L.L.C.
Publishing services by Front Edge Publishing

I dedicate this book, *God Incidents*, to the reader who has a God-tank right now that is running low or sits empty. I want to share with you ways to fill-it-up for your journey. I do so in gratitude for all those who have offered me roadside assistance and for the benefit of others who wish to render similar aid.

I also dedicate this book to God who I have come to love as the real author of life. Each chapter has led to deeper discovery and I look forward to what is yet to be made known.

Glenn M. Wagner

Contents

Foreword

THE WESLEYAN TRADITION is at home with
experiences of the Holy that transform life. Whether
remembering Charles and John Wesley or reaching back to
Christianity's earliest story of Paul's Damascus conversion,
history teaches of the living, continuing experience of God in
human lives.

I met Glenn Wagner in 1992 when he initiated a request
to move his pastoral ministry in the United Methodist
church from Illinois to West Michigan. His request
was motivated by concerns for his wife and his family.
That change led to a God incident for Glenn that you will
enjoy reading about in these pages.

In a backward glance most of us can recognize defining
moments when decisions are made that alter direction. The
move to Michigan for the Wagner family was such a moment
for them and has been a subsequent blessing for others who
have been influenced by Glenn's ministry. Glenn is an effective
pastor. The congregations he has served in Connecticut,
Florida, Illinois and Michigan have been beneficiaries of his
leadership. Glenn's learning and service in the Middle East,
China, South America, England, Scotland, and Taiwan have

stretched his spirit. Grateful parishioners and friends have supported an endowed scholarship in his name at Garrett-Evangelical Theological Seminary in Evanston, Illinois that has been helping others to pursue their calling into ministry.

Whether lay person or pastor, our days are filled with times of transition and change, fear and longing for comfort, anxiety and joy, belief and unbelief. Charles Wesley said about his experience on Whitsunday, May 1738 "the Spirit of God chased away the darkness of my unbelief."

You will find the stories and reflections of God-sightings Glenn shares helpful. God matters! At the deepest level human beings strive to experience and know Spirit beyond self. Wagner encourages and gives insights into how paying attention to God sightings along the way will enrich and strengthen life.

Looking back, we can see how important moments have influenced life direction. Your decision to read this book can be such a moment for you.

Sharon Zimmerman Rader
United Methodist Bishop, Retired

Introduction

IN NEARLY FOUR decades of pastoral ministry I have had the privilege of meeting many people who reject God. They disbelieve with strong reasons. Their authentic doubts have helped me to grow.

Steve was badly burned in a tragic auto accident prior to graduation from high school and endures crippling and disfiguring injury. His girlfriend dumped him after the accident and other friends left him, too. He survives on government assistance. Steve's rage against God, vented all over me, left a stain that can't be washed away.

Bill is a successful businessman. Bored with religion, he tired of personal obligations and moral restraint. Bill has given himself with new passion to sex and drugs. Bill abandoned his marriage and ran from his children. His callous indifference and the casualties of his choice opened wounds that have not healed.

Karen is a scientist. She is turned off by Christian fundamentalists and judgmental types who condemn her friends for their sexual orientation. I am challenged by her grace and by her reasoned disbelief.

Sarah is also done with God because her son, born without a skull cap, lived for 20 minutes after birth, then died. The trauma caused her marriage to fracture. Sarah is now aging, childless, alone, and bitter. Her grief is real. I wept with her in the delivery room and still grieve about what has happened to her.

Persons like Steve[1], Bill, Karen, and Sarah challenge me. They have caused me to stretch my understanding of faith. They have humbled me. They have taught me to listen – to them and to God. Their real questions about God are legitimate. Their attitudes about God are increasingly commonplace.

Are you also one of the growing numbers who have been turned off by your experience with God? Has your faith been jaded by hypocrites masquerading as believers? Are you disbelieving in God because you have been victimized by life? Have you been dissuaded from belief by show business treatments of faith that portray believers as backward, ignorant, superstitious, and bigoted? Are you one from the growing number who list *none* as your religious preference, and who currently neither know nor want to know God? Can you identify the reasons for your disbelief or disinterest? I wrote this book as a personal and pastoral response to Steve and Bill, Karen and Sarah.

But if you answered "yes" to some or all of the above questions, then know this book is for you, too. I believe that you will find this book helpful if you are a believer honest enough to struggle with doubt. You will also want to read this book if you have a desire to be more helpful to those you love who have given up on God.

Consider this your invitation from a friend to an open house. Briefly set aside your objections to faith. Give voice to your personal issues. Honor your doubt. Know that your questions are legitimate. Your feelings are real. But

---

1 The stories and quotes throughout this book are true. Contemporary names have been changed in many instances to protect privacy.

do not let your doubt keep you from re-engaging God in person. Suspend judgment long enough to take a fresh look at faith. This is a no-obligation offer. You can slip in to the meeting unannounced like an anonymous Internet surfer eavesdropping on a website. Why bother to give God another look? This meeting may change your life for the good.

I believe there is a creative, active supreme being many people call God Who is often made known to us in events that in this book are called God incidents. The first chapter of the book will define God incidents. Subsequent chapters will help you see some of the ways God is at work in the world, and may help you to respond to these ways. You will read of God incidents in the Bible and learn how our spiritual ancestors were changed by those experiences. You also will read contemporary stories of real-life God incidents that reveal what others are learning from God's messages.

Intelligent human beings disagree about God incidents. What one person may experience as a clear communication another may see as a mere coincidence or ignore altogether. You may have good reasons to be a skeptic. Perhaps you prayed for healing and your child died, or you tithed your earnings to a charity and your business failed. This book will address frustrating experiences when life does not turn out as we planned. Read further and remain open to discovering God at work in your own life.

Try this: picture yourself as a nomad living a century ago in the great empty quarter of Saudi Arabia, riding a camel atop a vast dune. In that bygone era you would have been totally ignorant of the truth that lying within reach, beneath the sands under your feet, was the world's largest supply of oil. Without the benefit of experience, even if you had been told of such a treasure, you might not have been able to understand its potential. Today, as a direct beneficiary of oil, can you imagine now choosing to live without it? If you were told today that there is a gusher waiting to be tapped on your own property, would you not be motivated to use that knowledge for your benefit and for others?

Like the nomads of yesteryear who were unaware of the potential at their feet, many today are unsure how to connect with God. God incidents help us to discover heaven at work in our midst. Knowing where and how to look for God can kindle deeper faith and open up divine lines of communication. Growing a living relationship with a loving God will help you discover spiritual purpose. We live life differently when we live it with eternity in mind.

As you reflect on the God incidents recounted in this book, I invite you to step from your current place toward a deeper connection with God.

Each chapter has been inspired by two realities that are part of life. On one hand there is real pain and disappointment in the world that can challenge faith in the goodness of God. On the other hand God is seen in many amazing ways. God incidents inspire many to believe in God and to live in faith despite life's challenges. This book recognizes that bad things happen, but it also demonstrates that God is still part of life. Just as a good optometrist can help a person with blurred vision with a new prescription for corrective lenses, my aim is to offer an alternate, improved perspective to those who feel cut off from God.

Questions to encourage reflection and discussion for each chapter are at the end of the book. Weekly readings are also suggested for those who wish to read this book as part of a study group. Different options are given to accommodate a variety of class lengths.

Because the life experience I have had with my sister Jane, which is described in Chapter 2, has been instrumental in formation of the ideas expressed in this book, a portion of the proceeds from each sale will benefit Lambs Farm in Libertyville, Illinois. Lambs Farm, a world-class community for adults with developmental disabilities, has been Jane's home for more than 30 years. I am profoundly grateful for their work. More information is available on their website at www.lambsfarm.org/ or by visiting them at 14245 W. Rockland Road, Libertyville, Illinois 60048.

CHAPTER I

GOODINCIDENTS

MORE THAN
COINCIDENCE

HAVE YOU EVER experienced a sequence of events that seemed to be more than coincidence?

In 1758, Benjamin Franklin published what may have been a much older proverb about a nail:

> *For want of a nail the shoe was lost, for want of a shoe the horse was lost; and for want of a horse the rider was lost; being overtaken and slain by the enemy, all for want of care about a horse-shoe nail.*[2]

Other variants of the proverb carry the consequence of the lost nail even further to include:

> *for want of the rider the battle was lost, and for want of the battle the war was lost, and for want of the war the kingdom was lost.*

The proverb is intended to remind us that little things do matter. It also points out the cause-and-effect relationship between seemingly unrelated activities, that, taken together, inspire us to marvel at the chain of events and say, "My, what a coincidence." One does not need to believe in God to agree

---

2 Benjamin Franklin, *The Way to Wealth*, 1758.

that what we choose to do with our lives can change the world in ways that can be observed and described.

In 1946, filmmaker Frank Capra created the unforgettable story of George Bailey (played by Jimmy Stewart) in the movie, *It's a Wonderful Life*. Bailey's life was given new hope when he was able to experience his town as if he had never existed. He learned firsthand how his absence would have had a negative impact on people he loved, and how his life had made a positive difference for many.

A coincidence is purely accidental and random, a matter of luck or chance, like the bouncing of lottery balls that select one winning combination of numbers from millions of possible options. There are moments, however, when events occur beyond an individual's control in such amazing ways that those experiencing them are right to give credit, not to random chance, but to God. It seems in those moments that heaven opens up and reveals to the human audience that God is really in charge. We give thanks for the glimpse of glory and are moved to worship with a greater awareness of God's presence. We may call these moments of amazing sequence "God incidents."

God incidents are similar to several other kinds of events that have been noted in literature.

Horace Walpole in 1754 coined a word, *serendipity*, to explain the reality of a fortunate occurrence or pleasant surprise. In a letter Walpole wrote to a friend, he described the discovery he made by reference to a Persian fairy tale, *The Three Princes of Serendip*. The princes, Walpole noted, were "always making discoveries, by accidents and sagacity, of things which they were not in quest of."[3] The idea of serendipity has been used to describe moments of surprising scientific insight leading to life-changing developments such as the invention of the telephone or the discovery of penicillin. Author Lyman Coleman used the idea of serendipity to train leaders in the art of using surprise. Coleman observed that using surprise

3 Horace Walpole, Letter to Mann, Jan. 28, 1754

can help group members move past natural obstacles to form meaningful relationships and grow into effective teams.

In the 1920s, Carl Jung, a Swiss psychologist, named a similar concept *synchronicity*, which he described as the experience of two or more events that are related in such a way that the person who experiences the events sees them as a meaningful coincidence.[4]

God incidents – in contrast to wonderful surprise (serendipity) or life-shaping insight (synchronicity) – deepen our awareness of God. God incidents help us to grow our faith in God. The Bible and life are full of remembered God incidents.

Acts 8 and 9, written by Luke and addressed to his friend Theophilus, give an orderly account of the early Christian movement after the death and resurrection of Jesus. Luke tells the story of how Saul of Tarsus became a Christian believer. Saul was an educated Pharisee, a law-abiding religious leader who was involved in the persecution of the early followers of Jesus. Saul was on his way to Damascus as the leader of a mission to arrest Christian believers for heresy when, suddenly, he was struck blind and heard the voice of Jesus calling to him: "Saul, Saul, why do you persecute me?" Disabled, Saul was led to Damascus by his anti-Christian companions.

While there, Ananias, a Christian, responded to prompting from God to go to Saul and to talk to him about Jesus. Unbelievably, this stranger, Ananias, walked into the home of people caring for Saul (the very man who was on a mission to arrest him) and proceeded to say to his enemy Saul the very words that would provide the evidence needed to convict himself! At a point in the story when we expect Ananias to be arrested, Luke reports instead a God incident. He details Saul's dramatic conversion to Christianity, his baptism, his recovery of sight, his name change to Paul, and his escape from the city.

---

4 C.G. Jung, *Synchronicity: An Acausal Connecting Principle.* Princeton University Press, Princeton, N.J. 1973.

It is clear that in the events leading to Paul's conversion, Luke wanted Theophilus to see more than random chance or happy coincidence. Luke sees God's hand in the incident of Paul's conversion. Consider that in the 2,000 years between Paul's change of heart about Christianity and today, nearly one third of the world's population, 2.1 billion people, identify themselves as Christians. Can you see the God incident in Paul's conversion, too?

Luke tells another similar, history-shaping God incident in Acts 10, recounting how Simon Peter, a Jew, dreamed about God's blessing foods that were clearly named as unclean in Hebrew scripture. His dream was followed closely by an invitation for Peter to dine in the home of an influential Gentile (non-Jew). Accepting the invitation was controversial because the meal was at the home of a high-ranking Roman officer, and the Romans were the occupying government in power oppressing the Jews. The Romans administered the crucifixion of Jesus. Romans did not follow Jewish dietary restrictions. Accepting the invitation could put Peter at risk of arrest as a known associate of Jesus. Breaking bread with a Roman official would certainly render Peter "unclean" to other Jews. During that luncheon, Peter, the first leader of the Christian movement after the death and resurrection of Jesus, made a declaration of significance:

> "Truly I perceive that God shows no partiality, but in every nation anyone who fears him and does what is right is acceptable to him."[5]
>
> **(Acts 10:35)**

In that revolutionary statement, Simon Peter set the Christian movement on a new trajectory, believing that God's love for all human beings is larger than the boundaries of our tribal groups. This landmark lunch, recorded in Acts and played out in history, is another great God incident.

5 All quoted biblical references are from the Revised Standard Version (RSV).

Today, God communicates with people in similar ways of amazing sequence to let us know of His love and desires for us. In 1992, my wife Nancy and I had come to a crossroads, and for personal reasons we needed to move to a new pastoral appointment. We sat down with denominational officials in Michigan to discuss a transfer from Illinois. Several weeks after that meeting, while Nancy was visiting her mother in her Michigan hometown hospital 300 miles away, the superintendent in Michigan phoned me in Illinois and offered a position as pastor in a city just 30 minutes from Nancy's parents. I called Nancy to share the news.

On her way out of the hospital Nancy remembered we would need child care during our Michigan interview. In a conversation she had had with her father that morning in the hospital, he mentioned her high school friend Ellen Smith had just bought a home in Nancy's old neighborhood. Following a spiritual nudge on her way out of town, Nancy drove by that house, wanting to ask Ellen if she could be available to baby sit. Nancy approached the house with confidence as there was a monogram initial "S" on the front of the screen door. She was surprised when the door was opened, not by her friend, but by an older woman she had never met.

"Oh, I am sorry to bother you," Nancy said. "I was told that my friend Ellen Smith lived here."

"You are at the right house, just a week early," the woman replied. "Ellen and her husband bought the home, and they will be coming here when we move out in a few days."

Nancy was prompted at that moment to say: "You know, I haven't been to this house in years. I used to come here as a child to take piano lessons."

"What a coincidence," the woman said. "My husband and I both teach piano and give lessons here, too. Would you like to see the house again?"

Nancy responded, "I'd love to."

During the tour, the woman asked Nancy: "I see by your ring you're married. Where do you live now, and what does your husband do for a living?"

Nancy said: "We live now in Illinois. My husband is a United Methodist pastor."

The woman said: "Another coincidence. We are moving because my husband recently got a new job as the organist and choir director at the United Methodist Church in another city about 30 minutes from here. Also, this very morning our dear pastor announced that he would be leaving the church for a new appointment. Just think, the new pastor doesn't even know it yet." Nancy thought: "*Oh, but he does, and I'm his wife!*"

In that moment, one woman observed a sequence of events that for her were a remarkable coincidence. Meanwhile my wife, Nancy, at the same time, in the same living room, was suddenly aware that she was part of a sequence of events that was far more than a coincidence. Just 15 minutes after receiving my phone call informing her that we would be moving to that same church, Nancy was standing in the home of a total stranger and experiencing a God incident. In that conversation, our anxious family found peace in the middle of a difficult decision because God was already in Michigan, getting a place ready for us to serve.

God continues to work in chains of events beyond our anticipation and control to let us know that He is in charge and that we are loved. We cannot plan on these events happening, but we can acknowledge them when they do occur, and we can live in humble gratitude for God's great gift of assurance.

CHAPTER 2

INCIDENTS

JANE:
A LIFE SHAPING
GOD INCIDENT

WHAT EVIDENCE IN life supports the idea that everybody counts in God's math?

When God chooses to be revealed, life is not the same afterward. A God incident that continues to shape my life has been the birth and life of my sister Jane. God has worked through her to teach important lessons. This is a real-life story that has God's fingerprints all over it. Jane's life has let me know that God exists and a bit about how God is at work around us.

Births are supposed to be celebrations of life. Expectant mothers often receive baby showers with encouragement and gifts that precede the blessed event. Birth announcements are sent out to herald the arrival. But not all births have happy beginnings.

Jane was born during the winter of 1962, the only girl in a gaggle that already included three active sons. She was born extensively brain-damaged, a condition complicated by a bad case of infant pneumonia. She went from delivery to intensive care. The family physician who delivered her was soberly pessimistic and did not expect her to survive that first night. To soften the emotional blow, she said, "Given your daughter's condition, an early death might be for the best."

At a moment when many parents are feeling the afterglow of the great joy that can accompany the birth of a child, Mom and Dad had to decide whether to continue care for Jane at the local hospital where she was delivered or to transport her by ambulance to a larger trauma center with more experience with high-risk infants. They chose to trust her survival to God and the locals.

Mom was exhausted from the delivery and still in the hospital. When Dad came home, he broke the news to us that our new sister was in a precarious medical condition. Then, Dad did something new for our family. It was not mealtime or bedtime or Christmas or Sunday in church, yet he suggested that we lift Jane in prayer. So, standing in a circle around our Formica-topped kitchen table, the Wagner men joined hands. Dad led the prayer, asking God to intervene so our newest family member would survive her serious medical issues.

The prayer on that unforgettable night was a petition of importance. Dad's plea to God came from a different place than the rote prayers of habitual faith. As he prayed, my 9-year-old self became aware of a larger presence in the room. I remember feeling comforted and at peace, though the news about Jane was to the contrary. As the Bible reminds us in multiple references, others have had similar mystical experiences with the Holy. A close encounter with God leaves an indelible impression.

The next morning, the doctor met with my parents and reported: "Your little girl has rallied. It looks like she's going to make it, but don't get your hopes up. Jane's brain damage is so extensive that she will be totally dependent on your care for the rest of her life. She may never be able to get out of bed on her own." Mom and Dad were coming to terms with the incredible change that Jane brought with her. They shared anxiety along with the looming unknown of raising a special-needs child. Heartfelt prayers for Jane became part of our daily routine. My parents shared the bittersweet news with their extended family and friends, and they, too, added Jane to their prayers.

In spite of the grim prognosis, my parents never gave up hope. Following Jane's extended stay in an incubator, we welcomed her home with caution. For a long time my brothers and I did not know how to handle Jane, but it was immediately clear that change was afoot. Mom's attentions were focused on our sister. Suddenly, more chores were added to our daily routine. Thanks to Jane, we learned how to do dishes and fold laundry, clean the basement, and weed the garden.

When Jane first came home, Mom was very protective. Gradually, we all adjusted to the new life in our midst. Mom grew more comfortable with her care, and we took turns holding her in the rocking chair. Like any baby, our sister slept, ate, soiled diapers, and cried when unhappy. Unlike infants who became active as toddlers, Jane did not have the muscle control to move around on her own. When other children were learning to crawl and walk and talk, Jane's body was still mostly limp. During her early months at home, it was far easier to see grim medical predictions for her life than God's unrevealed plans for Jane.

Mom and Dad kept searching for help and for people who had experience treating brain-damaged infants. They felt fortunate to be accepted as part of an experimental program at a nearby children's hospital in Chicago. Doctors there knew that in a healthy child an early important developmental step is learning to crawl. Physicians had learned that the development of a normal child's brain is most dramatic in the first six years, and stimulating the brain with early opportunities for learning enhances the capacities for healthy growth later.

The doctors at the children's hospital worked on the hypothesis that if this early capacity for development was true for healthy children, perhaps brain-damaged children, too, could be helped in their growth through a program called patterning. Participation in the patterning regimen would require a major commitment to a new daily routine for an as yet undetermined length of time. Her therapy would become a priority for our entire family. Mom and Dad made the decision and asked us to help. It is easier to say yes to something major like this when you have no idea what the commitment actually means. But we all knew by this point that doing nothing was not an option. Mom and Dad decided to give the program their best effort, and the whole family joined in. Before long we had to expand the circle of support to include volunteers from the neighborhood and from our church family.

By moving Jane's body for her in a crawling motion, doctors hoped that new pathways would be patterned into Jane's developing brain, and she might learn to crawl and then to walk and talk. Our family embraced the experimental patterning program for Jane. Three times a day for five minutes at a time, 365 days a year for seven years, five partners gathered around my sister to manipulate her body and perform the physical therapy of patterning.

Jane's inert body was lifted onto a foam pad covered with a bed sheet that lay on top of the kitchen table where we had prayed for Jane. One team member was tasked with rotating her head from side to side. The four partners, two standing on each side of the table, were asked to move one of Jane's limbs in a synchronized crawling motion. The exercise never varied for days that eventually turned into years. Keeping a full team assembled, trained, and on schedule was a never ending responsibility for Mom, who became the head cheerleader, recruiter, trainer, and scheduler.

Daily, Mom lived with the reality of Jane. When Dad was at work and my two brothers and I were at school, Mom faithfully organized and trained the volunteer teams that staffed the patterning table for each of the three daily shifts. Our church family provided the bulk of the extras that Mom needed to perform the therapy. Together, in an unforgettable way, we learned the power, necessity, and beauty of the gathered Christian community. This team helped us realize through their faithful presence that even Jane mattered to God.

Mom participated in nearly every patterning session where she offered a cheering presence for Jane. Her love was the glue that both kept the family together, and Jane's patterning team working toward the goal that someday this child would crawl and then walk and talk. The promised land was Jane's development, and we could not see the end from the beginning. Mom adjusted her own dreams for her daughter and learned to love Jane, not only as she was, but also for the special gifts that Jane gave to our family.

Jane's initial prognosis was wrong. By the grace of God, and with the help of many, Jane eventually learned to crawl, then to walk, and talk, and read, and write. While other parents celebrated the achievements of their healthy children in such ways as making the honor roll and winning in sports, we marked other milestones for Jane, though far later. It was a big event when she learned how to feed herself. We rejoiced when she could control her bladder. Dad, an avid reader, put his engineering skills to work in organizing new activities for Jane. He developed flash cards to teach his little girl basic concepts of math and reading. Dad bought a mini-trampoline and worked with Jane as she developed the skills of bouncing and balance. He enrolled her in special swimming classes that helped Jane tone her muscles and learn basic water skills. It was a cause for great celebration when Jane, then a high school student in special education, was able to sit on the backend of a tandem bicycle alone for the first time and balance and peddle as a partner around the block. Dad discovered that when Jane made progress with physical skills, it seemed to open up new parts of her mind to grow her intellect. She grew a remarkable facility for remembering phone numbers and a rare gift of total love and acceptance for others. My sister learned how to enjoy herself in every moment and how to look forward to the next big thing in her life.

At age 21, wearing a white robe and mortar board, Jane graduated from her special education school. It seemed fitting to her family that Jane was in a class by herself because in our eyes she always has been "one of a kind." Her teacher praised Jane's accomplishments. Jane amazed us all by singing from memory, "Tomorrow" from the musical "Annie." She will never appear on "American Idol," but she sings, if not always on key, with passion that tugs at heart strings:

> *The sun'll come out*
> *Tomorrow*
> *So ya gotta hang on*
> *'Til tomorrow*
> *Come what may[6]*

Eyes in her graduation entourage were filled to overflowing with tears of joy. We could affirm a great truth that night: Jane is not a burden; she is a child of God.

Today, Jane continues to be a vital part of life for her extended family. She is a high- functioning, special-needs adult. Jane holds down a job and lives in a group home with a house parent as part of a world-class community for adults with developmental disabilities called Lambs Farm in Libertyville, Illinois. The story of Jane's life as an answered prayer is a God incident and testament to how God acts in the circumstances of our lives to teach us important life lessons. The pain at Jane's birth has given way to awe at what God has done. Over the course of Jane's birth and development, God has taught those who know her that life matters, everybody counts, compassion is a powerful force for good, and more: there is power in prayer and in the body of Christ.

The formative experience in caring for Jane was a significant influence in what my brother, Richard, and I believe to be our call from God to enter full-time Christian ministry. Jane's survival and her life are a continuing God incident for us. If proof is needed that God can work in people's lives to bring about remarkable change, my sister Jane is Exhibit A.

---

6 From "Tomorrow" by Charles Strouse and Martin Charnin, Charles Strouse Publishing, Edwin H. Morris and Company.

When our mother died, Jane asked to sing a favorite hymn from memory as a solo at Mom's memorial service. Her singing helped us to realize that the Lord goes before us into our future to prepare the way, and, occasionally, God gives us a place where we can pause to see again the wisdom and glory of God's hand in the backward glance at history.

These God incidents give us courage to travel around the next bend where we may not wish to travel, and where what lies ahead is far less visible. Jane chose to sing these words from "The Hymn of Promise" by Natalie Sleeth:

> "In the bulb there is a flower;
> In the seed, an apple tree;
> In cocoons, a hidden promise:
> Butterflies will soon be free!
> In the cold and snow of winter,
> There's a spring that waits to be,
> Unrevealed until its season,
> Something God alone can see."[7]

When a pebble drops in a pond, the ripples on the water radiate out from the point of impact in ever-widening circles, leaving the spectator to marvel at the pebble's greater reach. The God incident of Jane's life has, over time, expanded from a prayer in a moment of uncertainty into a much greater living testament to God's grace.

"In the bulb there is a flower … unrevealed until its season… something God alone can see." And when, after years of painstaking nurture, the bulb blossoms and grows, and we are finally allowed to see the miracle of that flower, the blooming of God's glory takes our breath away and inspires heartfelt worship. Jane's life is a God incident that has helped me and those who have known her to recognize that God does work in our lives.

---

7 From, "The Hymn of Promise" by Natalie Sleeth, Hope Publishing, 1986.

CHAPTER 3

MIRACULOUS

GOD INCIDENTS

WHAT DO MIRACLES teach us about God?

God incidents are made known in many different ways. We observed in the first chapters that God can be made known to us through amazing sequences of events. When a God incident occurs, it causes us to take notice of God, like a neon billboard along life's highway. A second type of God incident that seems most prevalent is one that people of faith call a miracle. A miracle inspires those who experience it to look beyond cause-and-effect explanations to give thanks to God. Miraculous God incidents are often remembered as occurring quickly. They can bring about a dramatic change of fortune for the good, leading to spontaneous praise of God. Miracles also have been credited with life-changing behavior that follows the incident.

Miraculous God incidents are not new. The Bible records many God incidents of a miraculous nature. In Exodus 14, the people of Israel, freed from centuries of slavery, were making a hasty exit (exodus) from Egypt and were being chased by an Egyptian army determined to take them back into captivity. The Israelite position was vulnerable. They were trapped without defenses between a determined, well-armed force and the sea.

The Bible remembers in vivid detail the well-known God incident of the grand parting of the sea. The story tells the Israelite's hurried escape through the waters. It climaxes with their enemies, the Egyptians, chasing them into the parted sea. The passage closes and drowns the pursuing Egyptian army. Exodus 15:1 gives voice to the victory song that commemorated the occasion for the surviving Israelites:

> "I will sing to the LORD, for he has triumphed gloriously; the horse and his rider he has thrown into the sea."

Without doubt the Israelite survivors remembered that incident as a miracle from God. That God incident, like a shot of adrenaline to the newly freed slaves, gave an immediate boost to faith.

This miracle has been remembered by many during subsequent periods of difficulty, renewing trust that God would help them through their challenges. Words to a familiar spiritual capture the sentiment of how a remembered God incident, like the parting of the waters, functions for persons of faith whose beliefs are being tested:

> "I don't feel no ways tired, I've come too far from where I started from. Nobody told me that the road would be easy, I don't believe He brought me this far to leave me."[8]

Sometimes we may not be able to recall what we were doing three weeks ago on a Tuesday. By contrast, God incidents often carve themselves permanently into memory. God incidents, like an internal spiritual mapping system, can help to guide responses to life's challenges in the future. God incidents remind us who God is and how God cares for us.

---

8 Harry Thacker Burleigh, *I Don't Feel No Ways Tired*, Ricordi, New York, 1917, public domain.

In the biblical account of the Exodus from Egypt, it is clear that by itself, however, this life-changing, sea-parting, miraculous God incident was not enough to bring about a permanent condition of unwavering faithfulness in the Israelites. A victory celebration followed their successful crossing of the Red Sea and the defeat of the Egyptian army. This party is described in Exodus 15. We are told in three verses following the account of the party that the people had to journey three days in the wilderness without water. Rather than trust in God to continue to provide for their needs, the people began to grumble against their leader Moses.

This biblical memory of a miraculous God incident and exuberant faith, followed by hardship and doubt, shows a pattern of human behavior that is still evident today. We, too, are capable of believing thankfully that God has touched our lives. But we are equally capable of doubting God. In the moment of miracle we can thank God, but we also may experience restlessness or doubt when things do not go our way. Many of us want God to respond to all our needs as they occur. We want a God who, like a short-order cook at a restaurant, prepares our meal instantly to our personal tastes. Experience has taught me that God doesn't work that way. God has given us life, creation, forgiveness, and hope.

God's love for us is like a mother who donated a kidney so her daughter could live. What would we think of the daughter if she kept questioning the depth of her mother's love with the line, "What have you done for me lately?" Whenever they occur, God incidents are expressions of divine love that can engender deeper faith. They are gifts of God's grace. According to Christian belief, God has already given sacrificially through His Son and does not need to keep proving affection. Understanding that a God incident is a gift from God, given at God's discretion and in God's own time, can help us with patience when we do not get every wish fulfilled. When things do not go as we desire, we can look for the lessons that our challenging circumstances may be teaching us.

In the remembrance of miraculous God incidents, the Bible is honest that the same incident that sparks faith in some can be met with disbelief by others. John 9 tells of a miraculous God incident involving Jesus and a man born blind. In an event that led directly to a life-changing faith in God, the blind man's eyes were healed by Jesus. The newly sighted man became bold, praising God and telling others publicly that Jesus had healed him. Surprisingly, the healed man's testimony was rejected by Pharisees. These religious leaders were not willing to admit that a healing such as this was done by God because it violated customs that did not allow work on the Sabbath day. Before his healing, the blind man had been prevented by his disability from full participation in the religious community. But rather than being accepted back into the community, the healed man was rejected by religious leaders who themselves were blind to the miracle of the healing. The former blind man's testimony, grounded in the truth of his new sight, never wavered:

> "Why, this is a marvel! You do not know where Jesus comes from, and yet he opened my eyes. We know that God does not listen to sinners, but if anyone is a worshiper of God and does his will, God listens to him. Never since the world began has it been heard that any one opened the eyes of a man born blind. If this man were not from God, he could do nothing."
>
> **(John 9:30-33)**

Miraculous God incidents can spark renewed faith in God. Anyone might have one. They are not confined to the pages of the Bible. God remains involved, and miraculous God incidents continue to occur, inspiring new believers. Medical healings often are cited as evidence of divine intervention. When a healing defies conventional medical explanation

or when it moves people to give thanks to God, we call the
healing a God incident.

Cliff's miracle is a God incident. Cliff was sent home from
a major medical center with a terminal diagnosis of advanced
pancreatic cancer. Several of the world's finest oncologists
agreed. Cliff was dying. Treatments were ineffective.
Laboratory tests were conclusive. Cliff's doctors admitted that
there was nothing more that could be done to stop the rapid,
total, and inevitable advance of the disease, leading Cliff to
death. At best, doctors gave Cliff several weeks. Cliff, resigned
to his fate, stopped the aggressive treatments and returned
home, weak and jaundiced, to get his affairs in order. He
enrolled in hospice care, began making his funeral plans, and
called his family home for his last goodbyes. He looked and
acted every bit like a man who had but a short time to live.

Cliff's church surrounded him with prayer. They provided
Cliff with a prayer pager to wear on his belt. When people
of the church prayed for him, they would end the prayer by
dialing the number of the pager on their phones, causing the
pager to vibrate. Cliff never knew who was praying for him,
but the vibrations let him know he was being lifted in prayer,
often. After a year, hospice released Cliff from their care. He
lived for five years longer than the medical experts predicted.
His only medication for the pancreatic cancer was prayer. For
Cliff and his church, his continuing life – well past the best
medical predictions – was a God incident that grew faith in
God within Cliff, his family, and his church. People who knew
Cliff and his story found reason to share his good news as
evidence of divine intervention, and they were more willing to
relate their own personal needs to God in prayer.

For every cherished incident of divine healing, like Cliff's,
we also can tell stories of loved ones for whom prayers did
not lead to healing. Death and disappointment are a part
of life's experience. Believing in God and keeping God's
commandments will not shield us from hardship, nor
guarantee that miracles always will occur to rescue us from

loss. However, I would argue that, as a general rule, faithful living is more likely to produce healthier families and communities than does living with utter disregard for godly expectations. Majoring in love, practicing compassion, living in hope, and agreeing to live by God's commandments all help communities to flourish. While faith does not guarantee a difficulty-free life for the believer, faith does assure the believer that difficulties need not be faced alone.

Miraculous God incidents do occur. It is an aware person who acknowledges this gift, gives credit to the Giver, and responds to such an incident with a deepened commitment toward living in grateful faithfulness. God incidents can lead us into an ever-deepening relationship with God, who is the source of our life and the foundation of our hope.

CHAPTER 4

INCIDENTS

IN

SURPRISE PACKAGES

HAVE YOU EVER been surprised by God?

Amazing sequences and life-changing miracles are two ways we have seen that God is made known. We may think we know who God is, what God is like, and how God operates. Yet, God is full of surprises. When it comes to understanding God, we humans are often like the six blind men of Indostan, noted in the famous 19th century poem by John Godfrey Saxe, *The Blind Men and the Elephant.*[9]

In the poem, one of the blind men feeling the side of the elephant was convinced that the animal was very much like a wall. Another blind man feeling the elephant's trunk insisted the beast was like a hose. A third blind man feeling the elephant's tail swore that it was like a rope. Yet another embraced the elephant's leg and said the animal was more like a tree. Each blind man argued that his view was the absolute truth. But he had only a small part of the full picture. If given eyes to see the entire elephant, each blind man would stand

---

9 John Godrey Saxe, *The Poems of John Godfrey Saxe*, Complete edition, James R. Osgood and Company, Boston, 1873, pp. 77-78.

amazed that the whole truth was larger than his original vision.

Similarly, we know God is more surprising and more complex than an elephant. Our weak attempts to describe the nature of God are at best incomplete. Because of our inability to see God totally, we should not be amazed that God incidents often come in surprising ways that we never could anticipate.

Early in my ministry, I was surprised how God used an unlikely agent to remind me of God's amazing grace. I was preparing to go to my first pastoral job interview. A tall-steepled church in central Connecticut was looking for a 20-hour-a-week youth pastor. Anxious to make a positive first impression, I dressed for the interview in a new three-piece suit, taking care to put a fresh shine on my black leather dress shoes.

I had taken time to wash our car, but I need not have bothered. As soon as I got in the Chevy for the 20-minute drive to the interview, the heavens opened and soaked the earth in a torrential rain. The car wipers worked furiously as I drove the first blocks of the journey down the steep slope of Canner Street hill and turned left onto Whitney Avenue, now under three inches of a fast-flowing mini-river being fed by the rapid runoff from the hills above. I had gone about half a block when I heard a loud clunk followed by the sound of dragging metal on pavement. Something serious had just gone wrong under the car. I was ill-prepared for the rain, had no experience with auto repair, and was under a deadline for a job interview. What else could go wrong? I exhaled a prayer of desperation, "Oh, Lord, really?"

I pulled over to the far right lane, put on the car's emergency flashers, and stepped out of the car after climbing across the front seat to exit on the curb side. My shoes were immediately flooded by an ankle deep torrent, and my suit was also getting soaked. I peered under the car and saw the problem immediately. The entire exhaust system had fallen off and was lying on the pavement beneath the car in the fast running stream. Feeling helpless, I got back in the car and slumped in the seat, repeating my prayer, "Oh, Lord, really? What am I going to do?"

At that moment there was a rap on the passenger-side window. I looked up from my prayer, and outside my window was one of God's great surprises.

"Hey, mister. My name is Earl. You look like you need help."

I cracked the window and said: "You could say that. I think my exhaust system somehow became detached and is lying under the car. I don't know what I'm going to do."

The stranger replied without hesitation: "I can help you, if you'll help me."

I looked him over. Earl was wearing an open leather vest with no shirt beneath it to cover his numerous biker tattoos and the thick covering of body hair on his already sodden body. He was wearing blue jeans and flip-flops, and sported a pierced ear. He also was balancing an aluminum beer keg on his right shoulder.

In wonderment I asked: "What can I do for you?"

Earl replied without hesitation: "I've got some wire in my pocket, and I believe I can fasten your exhaust system back under your car so you can drive it until you can get it fixed later. If I do that for you, I'd like a ride about five miles straight up Whitney Avenue to the package liquor store, so I can return my beer keg and get my deposit back. We had a kegger at my place last night."

I said: "You've got yourself a deal."

Earl lowered himself beneath the car and was immediately soaked in the river running under the vehicle. I got out of the car to watch. It was while he was on his back lying under the car that I noticed the handgun Earl had wedged down the front of his pants. I feared the worst, imagining the headlines when the search party recovered my dismembered body, and my Chevy turned up in an East Coast chop shop after

being sold so Earl could host another kegger. But I was in no
position to go back on my word.

Quickly, Earl finished the job of wiring the car's exhaust
back in place and climbed into the car holding his empty keg
on his lap. The ride to the liquor store was the longest of my
life. Fears of a relapsed exhaust emergency were secondary
to my worries about Earl and my feeling like an accessory to
his lifestyle choices. The rain continued unabated and further
reduced security. To make small talk, I asked Earl what he did
for a living.

Earl boasted: "I don't do nothing. I'm into the three B's."

"What are the three B's?"

"Booze, broads, and ballistics," Earl said as he patted his
handgun proudly.

Earl did not ask me what I did. We rode the rest of the way
in silence.

When we arrived at the liquor store, I thanked Earl for his
kindness. He thanked me for the ride. I hoped that nobody on
the interview team was watching as their new youth pastor, on
his way to be interviewed, dropped off a biker and an empty
keg.

To this day, I am convinced that Earl's intervention in my
life at my moment of need was no accident of random chance.
Rather, it was a God incident of great surprise.

The Bible contains many stories like my encounter with
Earl where God incidents occur with the help of surprising
agents. One of these great surprises can be found in the
Old Testament book of Isaiah. In 586 B.C., Babylonian
King Nebuchadnezzar and his armies conquered the city
of Jerusalem and took the Judean survivors into 49 years of
slavery in Babylon.

The defeat of Jerusalem was devastating to the national
identity of the people of Judah. Those who survived the loss
and the slavery in Babylon had believed that the God who
created the world had entered into a special relationship
with them. They also believed that the land they possessed

was theirs as a gift from God, and that descendants of their late and cherished King David would continue to rule in an everlasting dynasty. The Babylonian defeat of Judah caused a major crisis in their religious convictions. Did the defeat mean that their God was weak? Did the end of rule by David's descendants mean that God's promises could not be trusted? Was the belief in an eternal relationship between God and the nation an empty lie?

This religious identity crisis was resolved when prophets declared that the defeat was God's punishment for unfaithful living and indifference to the poor. In essence, 49 years of slavery in a foreign land was understood as God's punishment for great unfaithfulness, the equivalent of a contemporary parenting strategy with disobedient children known as "tough love."[10] Much of the Bible portrays God as a loving parent concerned for his or her family's welfare. God promised kindness to the Israelite people, but He also warned them of the dire consequences that follow unfaithfulness.

The prophets of the Old Testament saw God's handiwork in their surprising history. They not only argued that the Babylonian victory was because an angry God allowed it, but also later declared that an unlikely candidate, the Persian ruler Cyrus who defeated Babylon and returned the Judean captives to their native Jerusalem, was God's chosen instrument (Isaiah 44 or Ezra 1).

Praise for Cyrus from Jewish religious leaders of the day is surprising because Cyrus was neither a priest, nor a king who descended from David, nor a circumcised Jew. Cyrus was the king of Persia. He conquered the Babylonians and his policies allowed for the Jewish slaves in Babylon to return to Jerusalem. The prophets declared that this non-Jew was being used as an instrument of God to fulfill God's purposes for the Jewish people.

Nor was Cyrus the only unlikely person to be used by God in the Bible. In the book of Jonah, we discover that God

---

10 Phyllis and David York, *ToughLove*, Random House, 1997.

used a reluctant prophet Jonah, an Israelite, to preach to the
Assyrians in their capital city of Nineveh. The Assyrians and
the Israelites were mortal enemies. It would have been unlikely
for orthodox Israelites to consider that God's circle of concern
included Assyria. In the climax of the book, we are surprised
to learn that the God of Israel cared deeply for the Ninevites,
too (Jonah 4).

In the New Testament Gospel of Luke, Jesus also lets us
know that God works in surprising ways. In response to a
question by a lawyer regarding requirements for inheriting
eternal life, Jesus tells the now-familiar story about the Good
Samaritan. In this tale, a traveler on the Jericho-to-Jerusalem
road is waylaid by bandits, beaten and left to die. The victim
is ignored by passing priests, who by virtue of their religious
jobs might have been expected to give assistance. Finally,
however, aid is given by a Samaritan who helps bind the
wounds, gets the victim to a place of rest, and pays the bills
for his lodging. This story stirred up controversy. Jews and
Samaritans have a history of conflict. Calling a Samaritan
good in an audience of Jews had to raise hackles. Criticizing
religious figures who blindly overlooked the opportunity
to assist a man in need elevated tensions. A contemporary
equivalent might be for Jesus to tell a story about a good
Republican during a Democratic political rally.

These biblical memories underscore a truth about God
incidents that still applies: God regularly surprises us by using
unlikely persons to serve as agents for divine goodness.

If God can work through Cyrus, the Ninevites, a Samaritan,
and a biker named Earl, then – surprise – God can use even us
for sacred purpose if we are open to the opportunities to serve.

CHAPTER 5

GOD INCIDENTS

AT THE

SCENIC TURNOUT

LOOKING BACK OVER your own life journey, can you identify God incidents when your life took a significant turn?

If you doubt God's existence, know that I can identify with your doubts. There are moments in life's journey when it may be impossible for us to see God's presence at all. In those moments we may have to journey quite a distance before we get a different view.

A 50-mile stretch of road in northwest Montana in Glacier National Park crosses the 6,646-foot high Logan Pass. The road is aptly called Going to the Sun Road. Construction on this winding route over the Continental Divide began in 1921 and was not completed until 1933. The road gives the term "highway" an entirely new definition. It is an engineering marvel featuring tight turns, steep drop-offs, and some of the most spectacular scenery in the world. Waterfalls, glaciers, alpine lakes, lush forests, cascading rivers, flowery meadows, and snow-capped peaks make each section of the journey a vivid memory. Driving here can be a white-knuckle experience. Guard rails are not always possible at the edge of the road. At the summit, a path from the rest area leads to an

awe-inspiring panoramic view of God's created majesty, one
that cannot be enjoyed at lower altitudes.

Likewise, some God incidents are seen only after a difficult
trip when the glory of God is shown suddenly from the
heights by looking back over the road that has been traveled or
by looking forward to the road ahead. In the Bible, Matthew
begins his retelling of the story of Jesus with just such a scenic
turnout view. As he looks back on Israelite history Matthew
tells how he believes that Jesus is God's son by first tracing
Jesus' family tree. Fourteen generations from Abraham to
the great King David, 14 generations from David to the
deportation to Babylon, and 14 more generations to the
birth of Jesus are remembered. Though readers may find the
retelling of genealogy puzzling at the start of a story, Matthew
does so to communicate his belief that God, whose existence
covers all of history, has had a miraculous hand in the birth of
this Jesus. He relates that Jesus is not just an ordinary person,
a random accident of history. He sees the birth of Jesus as a
God incident that is an important fulfillment of God's great
plan.

Matthew also ends his Gospel, fittingly, on a mountain
top in Galilee. The journey to that mountain peak passes
first through the arrest, trial, beating, crucifixion, and,
finally, resurrection of Jesus. It was not until the disciples
had experienced the trauma of losing their Lord that a risen
Jesus gave his close friends a view of God's road ahead. Some
biblical scholars feel that the site for Jesus' Great Commission
(Matthew 28) is the summit of the Arbel Cliffs. This high
point overlooks the northern end of the Sea of Galilee. The
breathtaking viewpoint from the cliff is a fitting place to
inspire Christ's disciples with a look ahead to God's dreams
for the world. In the Great Commission Jesus gives His
followers their disciple-making marching orders.

Matthew's Gospel is structured to begin with a look back
to the past in order to identify God's hand in the birth of
Jesus, and to end with a mountain-top view to the future so

Jesus' disciples can glimpse God's eternal direction. Having a sense of our ultimate destination can help us to find our way when we descend from the mountain to take the next steps of discipleship at lower elevations, where God's plans for the future are sometimes less visible.

We are keenly aware things can happen to us on life's journey which we do not understand. Misfortunes such as cancer, domestic violence, birth defects, persecution, and weather disasters can shake the foundations of our faith in a loving God. Hardships can discourage our willingness to invest in the exercise of faith. Yet, understanding that God can be known in scenic turnouts can help us to persevere with God even when our present is uncertain. We can trust in life's happy ending even if we are unable to see the future from our present place.

In his classic novel, *Les Miserables*, Victor Hugo uses the scenic turnout as a literary device to help us understand the sacrificial gift of God that changes his main character, Jean Valjean, from a bitter thief to a loving man. Hugo develops the character of kindly Bishop Myriel of Digne even before introducing us to Valjean. The unsuspecting reader is led into the life and heart of the bishop. When the plot has traveled the long and winding road and reaches a climax, we are made to feel exactly what is at stake when guilty robber Valjean is brought before the bishop for final judgment. Valjean steals from the one man in the world willing to give him hospitality, a meal, and a bed. Brazenly, he takes the bishop's valuables. The reader expects that Valjean will be resentenced to prison after being caught red-handed by the police. But instead of convicting Valjean, the bishop stuns the reader by redeeming Valjean. He gives the desperate and bitter man his prized silver candlesticks and a cover story that sets him free from the police for a whole new future. Valjean's moment of life-changing release from certain imprisonment, like the turnout on a mountain pass, invites the reader to see God's hidden hand and give thanks. Hugo's magnificent story inspires some readers to pray, "God, help me to grow like the bishop that I, too, may live with his kind of grace."

God incidents of the scenic-overlook variety are not just stories of a forgotten era. God still inspires faith with spectacular views. I can see God working across generations of my own family history. Over a century ago, my great-grandfather, Thomas Maris, died as a young adult of tuberculosis. Tom was a well-loved and respected physician who lived in the small Quaker village of Sylvania, Indiana. His premature death left behind a grief-stricken widow with two small children. Tom's young daughter was my grandmother. Jeanne Maris wondered in her diary, "Why?"

I do not know if my grandmother ever received an answer to her question about her father's death, but it is clear from where I stand, looking back over a century of family history since the death of Dr. Thomas Maris, that there are direct connections between his death and my life today. That loss dramatically changed the family's course in ways that led to my own life and development. My widowed great-grandmother married a Methodist circuit rider who moved his new family to the mission field in Montana. That new relationship ultimately influenced how and where my parents met and the faith they practiced.

British theologian Leslie Weatherhead, in his magnificent book, *The Will of God*,[11] suggests that while God does not cause many of life's difficult events to happen to us, God can use those instances, in a process Weatherhead calls "the circumstantial will of God," to reveal God's greater glory. God did not cause the crucifixion of Jesus but, over time, has changed the cross of Jesus' torture and death into a symbol of new life and hope. Weatherhead's observation about God's circumstantial will helps us to understand God incidents that can be seen from the scenic overlooks of life.

Such God incidents are helpful reminders when we are stuck somewhere, surrounded by trouble, and without a clear

---

11 Leslie Weatherhead, The Will of God, Abingdon, Nashville, 1944.

view of a way out. We can trust that God has the vast sweep of history always in view, and when the time is right, we might even get a glimpse of God's glory to remind us that our trip is worthwhile and part of God's greater design.

CHAPTER 6

GOD INCIDENTS

IN THE

GLORY OF CREATION

WHERE HAVE YOU experienced the awesomeness of creation?

Make a list of all of the reasons that you choose not to believe in God. You might include imperfect examples of human beings, biblical passages that are inconsistent with a message of divine love, a list of all your prayers that God failed to answer as you wished, and personal grief that is very real.

If you allowed me to offer a counter list of places where God has been made known, creation would be exhibit A.

God incidents are often associated with the glory of creation. Poets and artists, musicians and lovers have all received artistic inspiration from nature. In the Bible, Psalm 8 captures the joyful feelings of praise to God that can flow from the wonder of nature, "O Lord, our Lord, how majestic is your name in all the earth." Genesis 1 credits the act of creation to God, Who brings life into being and calls it good. Even scientists have been moved to faith in their study of the structures of life.

I once heard an astronomer from the Adler Planetarium in Chicago tell why he believes in God. In the language of science, I remember him saying our universe has been growing at the speed of light, 186,000 miles per second, since the first instant of creation. We can prove this by using light refraction experiments. The universe is made up of the same elements we read on the Chart of Elements that hangs on the wall of many chemistry classrooms. We know this from space exploration and the analysis of materials brought back to Earth to study. We find if we take certain elements and jolt them with electricity, amino acids form spontaneously. These are the basic building blocks of life. Thus, we can prove by science that life is built into the design of the universe. He concluded if some deranged person were to end life on Earth by starting a nuclear world war, it would be like someone taking an eye dropper and removing a single drop from the ocean of the potential for life that exists in our universe.

Care to be inspired by the universe? Check out the website www.scaleofuniverse.com. This site takes the viewer on a trip from a park on the Chicago shoreline out to far distances of the universe and then back again to see life through the lens of a powerful microscope. The journey provides a glimpse of the majesty and mystery of life, and gives foundation to the belief that life is designed by a being far greater than any of us.

In her book, *The Intention Experiment*,[12] author Lynne McTaggert chronicles a large and growing body of scientific evidence pointing to an unseen but still knowable spiritual dimension to life. It is possible for human beings through focused effort to interact with this spiritual part of life in ways that can be measured. Reviewing McTaggert's findings help us to understand God's majesty in new ways.

There are moments and places in our universe that inspire awe. Watch tourists coming for the first time to the rim of the Grand Canyon, or interview new dads in the delivery room at the hospital in the moment of the birth of a child. You can feel holy awe while traveling on a cruise ship in Glacier Bay off the coast of Alaska. You can read about this sense of wonder

12 Lynne McTaggart, *The Intention Experiment*, Free Press, New York, 2007

in the Internet postings from hikers on the Appalachian Trail. You can see inspirational pictures in an instant by typing "Biodiversity in the Amazon rainforest" as a search category on the website for Google Images. You can feel the glory of God by taking a quiet walk along a trail in a mature forest.

In their book, *Fearfully and Wonderfully Made*, authors Philip Yancey and Dr. Paul Brand explore the miraculous wonders of the human body and share with the reader their sense of God's presence in the very stuff of life. Brand describes the spectacular working of his own body in this way:

> *"I have closed my eyes. My shoes are kicked off, and I am wiggling the small bones in my right foot. Exposed, they are half the width of a pencil, and yet they support my weight in walking. I cup my hand over my ear and hear the familiar seashell phenomenon, actually the sound of blood cells rushing through the capillaries in my head. I stretch out my left arm and try to imagine the millions of muscle cells eagerly expanding and contracting in concert. I rub my finger across my arm and feel the stimulation of touch cells, 450 of them in each one-inch-square patch of skin."*[13]

Sailors who endure the fury of a winter storm in the North Atlantic, mountain climbers who ascend to the summit, and high-wire walker Nik Wallenda, who balanced his way across Niagara Falls and the Grand Canyon on a suspended cable, have spoken with eloquence about how the spectacular qualities of creation helped bring them to deeper faith in God.

The architects of the world's great houses of worship design these temples, mosques, and cathedrals so the art, acoustics, and space help the worshiper sense the majesty and mystery of God that is present in creation. Some of the most famous places of worship on Earth are built over the location where

---

13 Dr. Paul Brand and Phil Yancey, *Fearfully and Wonderfully Made*, Zondervan Publishing, 1980, pg 26.

a dramatic God incident took place. The building helps believers recall the incident. The Temple in Jerusalem, now the site of the well-known Dome of the Rock mosque, was built on the location where it is believed that Abraham brought his son, Isaac, to sacrifice him (Genesis 22).[14] Abraham spared his son when he used a ram caught in a nearby thicket as a last-minute substitution for the sacrifice. Similarly, the Church of the Holy Sepulcher in Jerusalem is located over the traditional site of Jesus' crucifixion, burial, and subsequent resurrection. St. Catherine's Monastery in the Sinai Peninsula is situated where many hold that Moses encountered God in the presence of the burning bush (Exodus 3). These are a few of the religious structures designed to help believers remember God incidents.

In 1886, a Swedish pastor, Carl Boberg, had a life-changing God incident in nature. Boberg, visiting a beautiful country estate on the southeast coast of Sweden, was caught suddenly in a midday thunderstorm. Thunder and lightning were followed by a brilliant sun and the calm sweet songs of the birds in nearby trees. The experience caused the pastor to fall to his knees in humble adoration of his mighty God. He described his inspiration in a nine-stanza poem beginning with the words, "O Store Gud." The English translation of his lyrics have touched millions of people who are similarly inspired by Boberg's God incident in the hymn of faith that some call the greatest of all time, *How Great Thou Art*:

> *"O Lord my God, When I in awesome wonder,*
> *Consider all the worlds Thy Hands have made;*
> *I see the stars, I hear the rolling thunder,*
> *Thy power throughout the universe displayed.*
> *Then sings my soul, My Savior God, to Thee,*
> *How great Thou art."[15]*

---

14 Note: Many Muslims believe that Abraham brought his eldest son, Ishmael, to the mountain to sacrifice him and not Isaac. J.M. Dent, *Koran*, Everyman, London, Surah 37:100-113, pg. 300.

15 Copyright 1953, renewed 1981, Manna Music, Inc.

If you aim to grow in your understanding and faith in God, if you are eager to build a relationship with the Author of life, then give yourself permission to experience the awe-inspiring qualities of creation. In those God incidents when you see the extraordinary genius of creation, let yourself feel the height and the depth, the glory and the breadth of God's awesome world. Then, in gratitude, live so that you bring honor to the Giver and the gift.

CHAPTER 7

GOD INCIDENTS

IN THE

WRESTLING MATCH

WHAT IS THE most significant issue you have ever wrestled with?

We have looked at some of the ways in which God has been made known: amazing sequence, miracles, from the scenic turnout, and creation.

Even so, there are many reasons for holding on to disbelief. Hostile feelings toward God can be rooted in painful experience. Doubt can be influenced by negative images of religious people, which air regularly in popular programming. Disbelief can be supported by personal study.

God incidents are not just experienced in the sunshine of answered prayer. We have all heard credit given to God by Olympic gold medal winners and Super Bowl champions acknowledging God's blessing for their achievements. When the ball bounces our way, and the good times roll, thanking God is easy. But God is not here only to paste a happy-face sticker on life; God is present also in real-life struggles. Some of the most important God incidents of all happen in life's darkest corners.

Early in my ministry, I worked as chaplain for an in-patient adult psychiatric facility. Part of my responsibility was to teach a class on spiritual growth for patients who struggled with deep-seated psychological and emotional issues. Some were suicidal and others clinically depressed. These mental health issues affected their relationships, their capacity to work, and their outlook on life. During class each patient was asked, "Have you ever felt close to God?" Most could describe a time when the love and grace of God was very real to them. Most remembered God incidents occurring when they were "hitting bottom."

One response was typical: "Once I tried to kill myself and was committed to the psych ward at the hospital. There I was stripped and put in a padded isolation room for my own protection. Then, when I could not fall any farther, I called out to God, and God was there for me. Through my tears I experienced God's peace, and knew that I no longer wanted to kill myself."

God incidents often happen in the midst of our difficulties. The Rev. Jim, then director of pastoral care for a psychiatric hospital, first asked the young person being interviewed for a job in the chaplaincy at the hospital, "Where are you hurting?" When the interview was over, the candidate asked, "Why did you ask me first about my hurt?"

The director replied, "Because I have come to believe that God can use our personal pain to create in us abilities to show compassion and empathy with others that do not get developed any other way. If you had told me that you have never experienced pain, I would not have hired you to work in this hospital because you would not be able to identify with, or minister to, the hurting persons who come here every day."

I learned with difficulty this unforgettable lesson about how God is at work even through our personal difficulty. I was a young associate pastor, serving at a large, vital church that was more than 100 years old. The senior pastor was a father figure for me and a valued mentor who offered me a monthly opportunity to preach to the faithful.

I learned in seminary preaching class that humor, appropriately used, can be a wonderful speaking tool to break the ice with the audience, establish rapport, and make an important point. What they failed to teach me was this lesson: Not everyone finds the same jokes humorous, and some can be offended by humor that misses the mark.

I do not remember the main point of my sermon that Sunday. I do recall being confident that my sermon was going to "hit a home run for Jesus" and inspire persons to new heights of faithfulness. At the outset of the message, I ad-libbed to try to establish a connection with the congregation. I poked gentle fun at the Russian Christians in our church who liked to sit in our balcony and were always "rushin' in" and "rushin' out" of church. The line got a nice laugh, and I proceeded to preach a sermon I thought was one of my best.

Monday morning in staff meeting, the congregation's long-time secretary said: "I hear you had quite a sermon yesterday."

I was pleased and responded: "Thank you. How did you hear?"

The secretary said: "I received a very angry phone call this morning from Mildred, who indicated that she won't be in to the office today to help with the newsletter because she was never so offended by anyone in the church as she was by your message yesterday. Mildred wanted us all to know she is quitting this church and never coming back."

Mildred and her husband were local farmers, 50-year members of the congregation, faithful attendees, and generous financial supporters of the ministry. They were regulars in the church balcony.

My ego deflated like a stomach hit by a full swing of a baseball bat. I felt sick with regret. I had not intended to hurt anyone. I certainly did not mean to offend Mildred. I immediately got in my car and drove to the Jones farm, all the while praying to God for the right words that could make amends.

Mildred, a tiny but formidable farm wife, answered my knock. She did not wait for me to finish my apology.

She said: "You hurt me deeply yesterday. I want you to leave right now, get off my property, and don't come back." She slammed the door in my face.

I was devastated by her reaction. I was not yet experienced enough to know that an intense reaction like Mildred's may have been triggered by a build-up of other issues in her life that remained hidden behind her closed door. I went back to the church and spent time in prayer. I wept with feelings of deep guilt that words of mine offered during the sacred time of preaching actually could drive a faithful person away from the church. A knot formed in my stomach that never went away. I distracted myself by keeping busy, resigned to the fact that I had been taught a difficult life lesson, and committed myself to being more careful about my use of humor. I resolved to work harder to be a better witness for Christ.

Mildred and her husband Ed did not return to church. Not a Sunday passed that I was not painfully aware of their absence. For weeks the front and center balcony pew, where they had been fixtures for 50 years, was noticeably empty. I felt the pain of a broken relationship, the internal call of Christ to reconcile, and the sense of helplessness that convinced me that I could not force Mildred to change her heart.

Four years passed. It was the beginning of summer. I was engaged in my free time painting our circa 1913 home. Having painted houses for a living during college, I was confident I could handle my own home. The house was two stories plus an attic and the rear of the building required some tricky maneuvering. I rigged a ladder, ladder jack, and some planking from the ladder that rested on the sloping roof, so it would enable me to cover more surface area of the attic and dormer without having to climb up and down the ladder so frequently.

Late in the afternoon, as I began to dismount, my scaffolding got out of balance with me on it. I fell from the top of the house nearly three stories to an ungraceful landing on my back. In the few seconds of the fall, my life flashed before my eyes. I suffered two compression fractures in my spine and the pain was excruciating.

The rescue workers carefully strapped me to a body board and moved me by ambulance to the hospital emergency room. Another ambulance followed us into the parking lot and unloaded its passenger on a similar gurney. With an equal sense of urgency, the other crew wheeled their charge through the doors alongside the emergency technician who was pushing me.

Mildred held her husband's hand as she walked alongside his gurney; Ed had suffered a heart attack and was being rushed to surgery. Mildred could not help but notice me. Our eyes met in that crisis, brought together in pain, to a place of immediate recognition. Suddenly, without a sermon, or coaching, or prodding, pride melted away. We both knew that the single most important thing in that moment was to be reconciled.

"Mildred, I'm so sorry," I said through my pain.

Mildred answered: "I'm sorry, too. We'll talk later."

Mildred and Ed returned to church. After many painful days, my fractures healed, and I did, too. The toxic, spiritual, and emotional waste that lingered for four years was washed completely away. I learned a powerful lesson: Reconciliation can happen, even when it seems impossible. God is at work, not only in creation and miracles, but also through our pain, teaching important lessons.

There are famous stories in the Bible that similarly remind us about God's presence in the difficult places of life. One such remembrance is the story of Jacob in Genesis 32. After cheating his brother Esau out of their father's blessing, Jacob had to run for his life. He went to live with his Uncle Laban, married two of his cousins, and had 12 sons and a daughter. Years later Jacob decided to return to his homeland to claim his promised family inheritance. On the way home, Jacob learned that Esau was riding out to meet him with hundreds of armed men by his side. Fearing that his brother was coming to kill him, Jacob sent his family and livestock ahead. What should he do?

During a sleepless night, Jacob wrestled physically with God. This dramatic God incident threw Jacob's hip out of joint, so he was ever after forced to walk with a limp. His crippling, and his later reconciliation with his brother, affected Jacob so much that he changed his name from Jacob to Israel, which means "One who has wrestled with God."

Wrestling or struggling with God is a common theme in the Bible that runs through the heart of the story of Jonah, a reluctant prophet. God commanded Jonah to go to Nineveh, the capital of Assyria, to preach to his and Israel's enemies. Jonah did not like the heavenly assignment to go to the East, so he fled to the West. Sailing away from a commitment to God didn't work for Jonah. As his ship was tossed about by a violent storm at sea, Jonah thought the storm was God's work. He urged the sailors to throw him overboard as the only way to calm the seas, but he was not able to escape from God by being tossed in the sea. He was swallowed by a large fish and remained there until he was willing to obey God's command. Though forced to do God's will, there is no doubt that Jonah's God incident changed his life. Jonah learned life-shaping lessons, not only about the will and power of God, but also about the grace of God.

Those important life lessons were learned not from a God who catered to the fears and prejudice of His prophet but rather from a God Whose messages to us can be contrary to what we really want to do. Jonah experienced God in one of life's difficult moments.

Another God incident that is remembered from a hard place is found in the Old Testament story of Job, a righteous man. Job was a living example of good fortune. He was healthy, wealthy, and beloved, living evidence for the frequent Biblical assertion that a righteous man will prosper. Then Job's life crashed. He disagreed with his friends and with God after his fall. He debated with friends who argued that his problems were because he was a sinner who needed to repent. Job insisted that his suffering was undeserved. He demanded to speak with God. God's answer to Job is the longest speech attributed to God anywhere in the Bible (Job 38-41). Surprisingly, God did not answer Job's questions at all. Rather, God raised the God questions that lead seekers to faith in the first place:

> "Where were you when I laid the foundation of the earth? Tell me, if you have understanding. Who determined its measurements – surely you know! Or who stretched the line upon it? On what were its bases sunk, or who laid its cornerstone, when the morning stars sang together, and all the sons of God shouted for joy?"
>
> (Job 38:4-7)

The God questions prompt us to a renewed awareness of our Creator's majesty, power, creative genius, and might. Job's struggle with both his losses and his meeting with God bring him to a deepened faith. This God incident also points us to a Lord who is with us in the midst of our misfortune. We are not to see bad luck as God's punishment for our sins. Job responded after hearing God, "I had heard of thee by the hearing of the ear, but now my eye sees thee; therefore, I despise myself, and repent in dust and ashes."

In his second letter to the Corinthian church, the Apostle Paul wrote about the ways that God was shown to him through the experience of great hardship and struggles. Should we mistakenly believe that loving God guarantees an easy life? Paul testified differently. Paul wrote that he was struck brutally for his faith on five different occasions, suffering beatings with rods and stoning. He endured three shipwrecks and survived 24 hours adrift at sea. Paul knew all about living in grave danger and the harshness of hunger and survival in the elements (2 Corinthians 11:24-28).

In that same letter, Paul wrote about additional hardships and about a thorn in his flesh that pained him so much that he asked for relief repeatedly from God. In answer to his prayers, God replied: "My grace is sufficient for you, for My power is made perfect in weakness." (2 Corinthians 12:8).

In other words, we should not be surprised when life challenges us with hardship, suffering, and disappointment. Horrific things can and often do happen to most of us, but it is also true that God is present even in the difficult moments of life. The God incidents that come from the wrestling matches are real life-changers.

CHAPTER 8

GOD INCIDENTS

GOD AT WORK

EVEN WHEN

WE DON'T KNOW IT

DO YOU THINK there are places where God is at work now that we are unable to see?

You may have solid reasons for disbelief. Life can be dangerous. People can be cruel. Real experience has caused some to subscribe to the law of the jungle, "Do unto others before they do it to you," rather than the Golden Rule, "Do unto others as you would have them do unto you." Faith in God will not immediately change the environments that shape this belief, but God can change us. Faith can change how we view the challenges life throws at us. Though we may be unable to change what happens to us, we can choose how we will respond. Experiencing a God incident can help us to change our outlook on life in much the same way that a satellite photo can change how we perceive the Earth.

Consider for a moment the art and science of cartography, the making of maps. Did you ever wonder how, long before satellites, mapmakers were able to give us accurate images of the Earth's surface? How did mapmakers ever figure out that the country of Italy is shaped like a boot or that the Lower Peninsula of Michigan looks like a mitten?

Many ancient navigational charts were made by sailors using a tool known as a sextant. With this device the mapmaker used the known position of the ship as a starting point, the fixed point of a star in the heavens, and then factored in the time and speed of a ship for a third point to measure distance. Ancient maps, charted with these old methods, sometimes appear to be crude approximations of known geographical features. Contrast the time-consuming, old style of mapmaking with today's methods. Advanced satellite images help us better know the shape of the land we inhabit. With confidence we can rely on today's maps to tell us both where we are going and when we have reached our destination.

Maps give us perspective on lands previously unknown. Maps can help a traveler to have a sense of the terrain ahead before it is even seen. In a similar way, stories of God incidents can help us to see God's working more clearly by giving us a big-picture view. Although God is always present and available, there are times when we do not see God's guidance and may be blind to God's activity in the present moment. But we must never discount the possibility that God's hand is a part of life.

The biblical story of Ruth is a helpful reminder of this important lesson about God working behind the scenes, unseen to us, but essential to the outcome. The story of Ruth opens with tragedy. An Israelite father and his two sons died in Moab, leaving behind three widows: the mother Naomi, and her two Moabite daughters-in-law, Orpah and Ruth.

We can identify with the widows because grief is an inescapable part of life. Had three family deaths within a short span of time happened to any of us, most would be unable to see God's hand in the midst of our loss. Rightly, we might be offended if an insensitive onlooker dared to declare to the widows that their misfortune was somehow God's will. Bad things do happen. Grief hurts. Loved ones die. No words are adequate to soothe the pain of loss.

The author of the book of Ruth has our attention as the story unfolds.

Naomi urged her widowed daughters-in-law to make new lives for themselves in their homeland. Orpah agreed with her mother-in-law and chose to return to her family in Moab. Naomi decided that she would return to Bethlehem and the land of her kinship ties. Rather than letting Naomi make the difficult and unsafe trip alone across the Jordan River and back through the wilderness, Ruth said to her mother-in-law: "Where you go, I will go, and where you lodge I will lodge; your people shall be my people, and your God, my God" (Ruth 1:16).

Ruth's statement of faith in God and her devotion to Naomi appear to be the only hopeful elements in a story full of grief. Two women alone, without employment and with no obvious prospect for survival, travel back to the older woman's ancestral home. It is remarkable that this family is remembered at all. Ruth's story in the Bible parallels many stories of sorrow that appear regularly on our nightly news, such as, "Children Shot," "Tsunami Lays Waste to Shoreline," "Nuclear Accident Devastates Region," or "Terrorist Bombing Takes Innocent Lives." Where is God in any of these disasters? At times, there is only one answer that is authentic: We don't really know where God is. Yet the book of Ruth reminds us that God is at work even when we are unaware of it.

God's working in Ruth's case is seen only because her story was written down. We can see God's involvement in this drama 3,000 years after the event. From Ruth's tale we read that Naomi helped her daughter-in-law catch the eye of Boaz, a kinsman. The marriage of Ruth and Boaz produced a son, Obed. He was the grandfather of King David, Israel's greatest king. To further see how God has worked through Ruth, more than 1,000 years after she died, the Gospel writer Matthew recalls how 16 generations later, a child named Jesus, a new king of consequence, was born.

It is fair to guess that Ruth, in the middle of her personal tragedy, had little awareness of God's working. However, looking back through history, we can see that had Ruth not decided to step out in faith to accompany Naomi from Moab to Bethlehem in their shared tragedy, Judeo-Christian history would have evolved differently. Ruth could not have known that without her devotion to Naomi there would have been no David and no Jesus. Erase both men from history, and the world would be a vastly different place.

This story about Ruth, a foreigner, was remembered in the Bible partly for her key role in the history of Israel's most important family. Her story also was remembered because later in Israel's history leaders such as Ezra and Nehemiah were passing laws demanding that Jewish men divorce their foreign wives. They insisted that a traumatic military defeat followed by forced enslavement were punishment from God because the Israelite people had chased after other gods. They blamed this punishment on the influence of foreign wives who introduced other gods to their families. These leaders reasoned that banning marriage to foreigners would be a way to keep religion pure and the people united in their worship of God. Ruth serves as a corrective counterpoint to Ezra and Nehemiah's reactionary marriage laws. The story of Ruth reminds us that God's grace is bigger than our narrow-minded fears. Not all foreign women were idolaters. Ruth was a foreign wife who played a leading role in our inherited story of faith.

Another important lesson from Ruth is that it is exactly in those moments when we have no idea what God is doing, or why tragedy strikes, that we should continue trusting in God.

Just as a view by satellite of a landscape or a map can help us to see where we are going, the hand of God is often most seen with a bit of distance between us and a crisis. When I broke my leg during a trip to Israel, I couldn't discern God's presence in the trauma. A broken leg changes plans. Instead of fulfilling a dream, I found myself flat on my back in a foreign country, wallowing in pain and self-pity. I was angry at God and at myself for what felt like a silly accident. I wished I could relive that moment with an ending that did not include fracturing my leg and surgery to repair it.

My views on the unpleasant circumstance changed when I asked a simple question: "OK, God, what would you like me to learn from this?" When I opened myself to the possibility that the broken leg was not just a random accident, God began to teach me important life experiences that have shaped my life and work. In the eight-bed ward that was my hospital room, I received valuable lessons about living in community from the four Jews and three Palestinians who were my roommates. We each came to the room with individual handicaps and different abilities, and we soon learned how each was needed to contribute to the welfare of the group. After returning home from Israel, I learned that many around us struggle with disabilities. Many of our public buildings, including my own church, were not accessible to persons with physical limitations.

My first day back at work after the accident was also a Communion Sunday. I had never before celebrated this sacrament while balancing on crutches. My right leg in its cast was throbbing when I got to the words of institution and the breaking of the bread. When I came to the part where I said, "Take, eat, this is my body broken for you," I choked on the words.

In that moment at the altar, thoughts about Christ's sacrifice and broken body flooded my consciousness. Who would willfully choose to be broken? Being broken is painful. My broken leg was expensive and inconvenient. It was disruptive. For Christ, broken meant laying down life itself. The only people who choose to be fractured on purpose are those with a deep love, who see that by being broken they can save someone else they love even more, like a mother who gives a kidney to save a daughter, or a soldier who throws himself on a grenade to save his comrades. I knew in that instant that I could never again in good conscience ignore, nor take for granted, such a sacrifice on my behalf.

I share these stories – about Ruth, about mapmaking, and about an inconvenient broken leg – to underscore the important insight that God is with us. We may not be able to recognize God's presence in the midst of a life crisis. Just as visitors to Michigan may be unaware that they are standing in the middle of a geographical mitten until they are able to see the whole peninsula in a satellite picture or portrayed on a map, we also may be blind to God's presence in a given moment. But the story of Ruth reminds us that we should continue to trust that in time God's overarching purpose will be revealed.

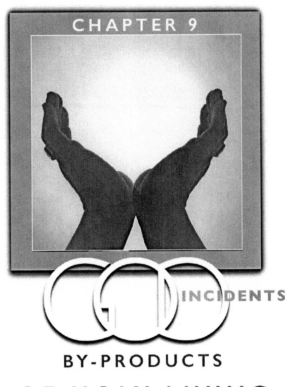

CHAPTER 9

GOD INCIDENTS

BY-PRODUCTS

OF HOLY LIVING

DO YOU THINK there are some behaviors that will bring us closer to God?

This book has been structured so that each chapter considers God incidents like a jeweler studying the many facets of a rare diamond. Each chapter views the subject from a different, illuminating angle. This chapter suggests that God incidents often can be experienced as a natural consequence of choosing to follow God's great commandments.

There is an amusing story about three boys standing on a hillside and boasting to each other about their wealthy fathers. The son of a rancher bragged: "My Dad is so rich, he owns all the land you can see to the east, all the way to the horizon." The second boy, not to be outdone declared: "That is nothing. My Dad is in real estate, and he owns every building on Main Street." The third boy was the son of a pastor. He boasted: "My Dad is richer than both of yours. My Dad owns hell."

"How do you know?" one of the other boys asked.

"Well, he came home last night from the church council meeting and told us that during the meeting he asked for it, and the board members gave it to him."

None of us needs travel very far to find a clear path to hell in our world. Hell can be encountered on the mean streets of poverty, in the smell of government corruption, in the ugly brutality of war, and in the toxic stew of prejudice. We might ask whether there is an alternate road map that can take us to another destination, straight to God. Can we obtain directions that, if followed, will lead us to have life-changing incidents with God? Many have come to believe that it is possible to live in such a way that God incidents are experienced regularly.

Attie taught an unforgettable lesson that confirmed for me that the choices we make and the life we lead do make a difference in how we experience God incidents. Attie, a 90-year-old widow, lived in a house with her daughter and grandchildren. The worship team at the church where I served was planning a Sunday service which would focus on the contribution of senior citizens. During the planning, the team asked me to invite Attie to lead the congregational prayers. I was skeptical that a 90-year-old would be able to contribute much as a substitute for a *real* pastor. The sin of pride was at work in me. Attie had had no courses in public speaking, had not attended seminary or even college. I was not even sure she knew how to use a microphone. I anticipated an awkward moment on Sunday when Attie came forward.

I was not prepared for the God incident that occurred as Attie slowly and gently got herself into position in the front of the church. This unlettered woman, whose worn hands and friendly behavior reflected a simple yet faithful life, bowed her snow white head before the Lord.

Attie's voice was soft but clear. Her prayer was not the polished prose found in books of prayer, nor was it the quick let's-get-this-done prayer offered by persons eager to move onto the main course at a dinner table. Attie's prayer was offered by a person who had spent a lifetime on a first-name basis with the Almighty and had a profound love for her God. She invited us into the royal throne room of God's grace, and we experienced her as a doorway into the very presence of God's holiness and love. When Attie prayed, the glory of God was revealed. We experienced a hushed reverence and were filled with awe. We felt the peace of God that exceeds understanding. We did not want Attie's prayer or our intimate time in God's presence to end.

What made this a God incident? It was Attie and the glory of God shining through her. I believe that what I experienced with Attie was something called congruence. When what we believe and what we say and what we do are in alignment, then our words communicate with a power that is not present when our words misrepresent the truth about us. In Attie's case, her words, and her lifetime of devotion, were aligned that morning with God's Holy Spirit. That life-changing prayer helped me to recognize that God can take up residence in each of us.

The Apostle Paul called this indwelling of the Holy Spirit a treasure in earthen vessels to show that the heavenly power belongs to God and not to us (2 Corinthians 4:7). This power of God shines through believers who seek to pattern their lives after the example of Christ. The presence of God burns even brighter in the life of a believer who lives intentionally, loving God for a lifetime. Attie was able to bring a congregation into the presence of God because she and God were on a first-name basis as a result of her decades of purposeful devotion.

I have been blessed on subsequent occasions with a similar awareness of God's life-changing presence during sermons by others. In each instance the speaker's words and the substance of his or her life were in alignment with a demonstrated devotion to God. I do not always know what moves others to incline their lives in a Godly direction. I do know I have made a decision to love God in gratitude for gifts received, in acknowledgement of God's greatness, in understanding that loving God leads to better consequences, and in a desire to emulate others whose living example has served as inspiration. I acknowledge that a decision for faith is not a one-time commitment that lasts forever but is a conscious choice which gets made and remade daily while dealing with life's changing circumstances.

John Wesley, a man who started a Christian movement that now extends to 159 countries and 80 million people, was a living example of how to live with self-discipline. Until his death in 1791, Wesley worked proudly to live as a Methodist, a derogatory name given by his detractors because he lived his life with method. Wesley's great desire was to focus on giving glory to God in every aspect of his living. He described his method as "living with a single eye,"[16] and he searched the scripture for directions for how to live an intentional life of faith. Wesley was convinced we do not come to God and stay with God by mere chance but rather through the intentional exercise of faithful habits. Wesley addressed this topic in his writings. He examined, among other things, how the words we speak, the books we read, the politics we endorse, the social policies we support, the investments we make, the alcohol and other drugs we ignore, the clothes we wear, the food we eat, the music we play, and the way we manage our time all can work to deepen our faith. Our actions can make it more likely that we will be aware of, and participate in, the God incidents of life.

Just as athletes prepare their bodies through disciplined practice in order to perform at top efficiency, and just as musicians spend years practicing their art so that their performance before an audience may fly to new heights, it seems reasonable that we can order life in such a way to be in touch more closely with God.

These behaviors are not just showy exercises in public holiness. The prophet Isaiah, for example, criticizes empty efforts to show piety and points out why certain religious behaviors have no impact with God. He notes that God is not interested in showy religion that is divorced from a life of faithfulness. He urges people to practice generosity to the poor,

---

16 John Wesley, *On a Single Eye*, Sermon 118.

be fair in their business practices, and rid their lives of gossip about the sins of others (Isaiah 58).

Jesus reflected the spirit of Isaiah with a memorable example of service when, during a sacred meal with his friends, he assumed the role of a household slave and washed his disciples' feet over their objections. He followed his living object lesson with a command: "As I have done for you, so also shall you serve one another" (John 13:34). The life of Jesus and his teachings suggest that committing oneself to humble service as an act of devotion to God will bring us closer to God as we experience life-changing God incidents.

Paul similarly experienced God incidents and encouraged holy behavior as a means to live in the Spirit of God. In one of his letters (Galatians 5), Paul urged believers to avoid indulging the desires of the flesh and proceeded to list behaviors that will lead persons away from God. By contrast to these sinful behaviors, Paul names "love, joy, peace, patience, kindness, goodness, faithfulness, gentleness, and self-control" as fruits of a spiritual life.

Richard Rohr, an author and Franciscan monk, similarly observed this truth about our capacity to experience and share God more completely through consciously choosing to live faithfully: "Happy and humble people finally change people, much more than ideas, sermons, or theology ever will. We must know that any encounter with a large or lovely life changes our imagination forever. We always henceforth know it is really possible. We are thus attracted forward."[17]

God incidents are often experienced by persons who seek a deeper relationship with God as a consequence of faithful living.

---

17 Richard Rohr, *Eager to Love* , Franciscan Media, Cincinnati, Ohio, 2014, p. 263.

CHAPTER 10

U TURN O.K.

GODINCIDENTS

IN THE DIVINE
REVERSAL

DO YOU THINK that faith can make a difference in the content and direction of life?

An honest appraisal of your life by an independent consulting firm may in fact agree with your own assessment. Your life may give ample grounds for disbelief, disappointment, discord, and discontent. You may even have reason to believe there is no cause to hope for any change on the horizon. But it is also true that for every life that is stuck, there are persons who share an equally honest assessment of how faith has changed things for them in a dramatic U-turn.

Of the many types of happenings human beings have understood as God incidents, some events stand out as dramatic changes: A greedy and corrupt tax collector becomes generous and honest. A blind man receives his sight. A non-believer becomes a convert. A sinner becomes more faithful. A liar tells the truth. In his or her 180-degree turnaround, the person showing the new behavior often points to a meeting with God as the reason for the reversal.

Alcoholics Anonymous is an organization filled with persons who can give personal testimony to the power of Godly change in their own lives. John was like many others who have made regular meetings of AA a personal priority. In a room crowded with persons from every walk of life, held together by a common problem, John stood and shared his testimony: "My name is John. I'm an alcoholic."

He told his story:

"I began drinking at an early age. Alcohol was a regular part of life at our home. Mom and Dad both drank at the evening meal, and alcohol was always present at family gatherings. Older cousins slipped me my first beer during a family reunion. Drinking made me feel grown up and less shy in social settings. In high school I found acceptance in a circle of underage friends. We felt like we were all beating the system by drinking years before it was legal. Several friends had parents who sponsored keggers for underage teens, thinking they would rather have their children drink under their direct supervision. Most of my friends and I didn't know how to quit drinking until the alcohol was gone. In college, I drank away my music scholarship and borrowed money to pay for tuition, spending it instead on my growing appetite. I liked the escape from my problems that alcohol offered, though I was aware that I gradually had to drink more to get the same pleasure. Some nights ended with vomiting. I experienced blackouts. Morning-after hangovers were horrid, but I kept on drinking.

"With a desperate need to find money to support my growing habit, I took a series of part-time service jobs at mostly minimum wage. I worked to drink, and I lived anticipating my next high. Even though I thought I was OK, I also learned the hard way that employers do not tolerate frequent absence, being late, weak excuses, and poor effort. Landlords expect rent to be paid. Bill collectors get ugly when debts are not covered. My drinking led me deeper into debt and eventually into homelessness. When I had fallen so far with getting high as my guide, it was easy for me to start begging and stealing. My life was reduced to a smaller world within walking distance of feeding programs and shelters.

"One night at a church-based shelter that required guests to attend a church program in exchange for a bed, a shower, and a hot meal, I heard another addict speak with deep feeling about new life in Jesus Christ. He told a story that sounded a lot like my own. He shared honestly about the help his faith gave to him. He spoke of living one day at a time and about the difference between a life of addiction and one of sobriety. For some reason, at that moment I felt like I had hit bottom. That sober alcoholic was speaking directly to my heart."

John had a divine reversal that night. He opened his heart to accept Jesus as his Lord and Savior. John still tears up when he remembers the feeling of peace that he experienced when he asked God for forgiveness and opened his life to serving Christ.

Today, John's life has been turned around. He has been alcohol-free for 15 years. He is married and has a son. John works as an alcohol counselor and shares his testimony of how a living faith in Jesus has changed his life for the better. John's life reversal is a God incident.

Charles Colson's story is another example of a man whose meeting with God led to a life change. Special counsel to President Richard M. Nixon from 1969 to 1973, Colson gained notoriety at the height of the Watergate scandal. He pleaded guilty for trying to defame Daniel Ellsberg (of Pentagon Papers fame). In his testimony, Colson readily admitted his role in trying to cover up the wrongdoing of the Watergate break-in on behalf of the White House. In 1974, he served seven months in a federal prison as the first member of the Nixon administration to be imprisoned for Watergate-related charges.

Colson became a Christian in 1973. His awareness of his own sinful behavior led to a conversion to Christianity. Colson had been part of a team that could call themselves the most powerful men in the world, with all the people and agencies of this great country willing to do whatever they asked of them. Yet the smartest people in the country were unable to cover up a crime and to lie for more than a few months before it all blew up in their faces. Colson noted the irony in an opposite situation: Jesus' closest friends, a poor, working-class lot, died as martyrs for their faith in Jesus' death and resurrection.

Colson said it was then he realized the only way people would willingly die without changing their story was if they were telling the truth.

He made a decision to believe in Jesus. His mid-life change led him to start the nonprofit Prison Fellowship, the largest prison ministry in the world, and to a life devoted to sharing his faith with others. Colson traveled the world as a public speaker, wrote more than 30 books, and hosted a daily radio show that was heard on more than 1,400 outlets across the United States. He received 15 honorary doctorates and, in 1993, was awarded the Templeton Prize for Progress in Religion. This million-dollar prize is given annually to a person who "has made an exceptional contribution in the field of religion."

Earlier we talked about the God incident that led directly to the dramatic change and conversion of the Apostle Paul, from enemy of Christ to one of his most important advocates. We know about Paul from the content of the 13 New Testament letters that are attributed to him, and from the description of his ministry offered by the writer Luke in the book of Acts. Without Paul's wise insights, essential Christian ideas – such as love, grace, the body of Christ, resurrection of the body, and fruits of the Spirit – would be missing or limited. Paul's desire to build new congregations and to emphasize the love of Jesus that included everyone – Gentile and Jew, male and female, slave and free – has given power to a global movement for God.

I have met people inspired by a God incident who have decided to make love a priority. They leave a different impression than those guided instead by selfish interests. Compassionate neighbors motivated by God incidents offer a different vibe to community than others who come and go with indifference. A basic teaching of Jesus is forgiveness, which is contrary to vengeance practiced in much of the world. Likewise, living in a faith community is very different from free-lancing as a lone ranger. Choosing to believe in hope for eternity contrasts with despair at death. Generosity, inspired by God's love, produces very different fruit than stinginess. Treating people with dignity, after the example of Christ, is a complete turnaround from rudeness.

Choosing to obey God's commandments voluntarily is a world apart from living with an "anything goes" mentality. Exercising God's grace toward those who are different from us is a reversal from being threatened by the world's many cultures. Gratitude for the gift of life and natural resources is far more satisfying than doing nothing to help prevent pollution. Believing in the peace of God beats living in constant fear stirred by the daily news cycle. Gratitude for creation feels like a better way for living than the alternatives that miss the wonder of life.

Faithful disciplines for living can grow healthier families, stronger communities, and happier people than war, addictions, or selfish enterprises. God created life to be lived in relationship with Him.

Under the category for guiding ideas, life offers each of us multiple choices. You do not have to go far to find persons peddling alternative beliefs. But if you judge an idea by its fruits, and you evaluate the long-term consequences of holding your convictions, then choosing to love and serve God is worth consideration. Choosing to love and serve God will bring about a dramatic change in thought and action. That change in our lives may not be seen as readily as it is in the life of a sober alcoholic like John, or in a world-changing missionary like Paul, but loving will turn our lives in a positive direction, thanks to God who inspires reversals.

CHAPTER II

INCIDENTS

IN THE NEIGHBORHOOD

WITH JESUS

HAVE YOU EVER been in a place where it felt to you that God was totally present?

On a scale measuring your perception that runs from far away on one hand to near and dear on the other, how would you describe your current relationship with God?

My personal conviction, grounded in my experience, is that God is always present, but we can put ourselves closer to where God has especially promised to be. We are more likely to experience God incidents if we serve as God has commanded in places where the Bible and experience has taught us that He can be found.

Aaron, our son-in-law, recently introduced my wife and me to geocaching, a sport for those who love the out-of-doors. The activity feels like a cross between Boy Scout map reading and a treasure hunt. Geocache enthusiasts hide items, then record coordinates on the Internet, so fellow hunters armed with cell phones or specially programmed GPS units can track and find the treasure. When the loot is discovered, geocachers sign their names in a log book, post their discovery online, and often add to the treasure, which is then re-hidden for the next seeker. On a first outing we found a cache hidden under a light pole near a funeral home and several more hidden high in trees in the middle of a forest preserve. Finding the treasure was great fun, but it required initiative, effort, a good map, and a compass. The search for the cache provided added excitement to a walk in the woods.

Experiencing a God incident is similarly engaging. You need willingness to hunt and a good map. Fortunately for us, the Bible offers many hints about where we will find God. We are more likely to experience a God incident if we intentionally place ourselves in the neighborhoods where Christ has told us He will be.

This important lesson about God incidents I learned in a life-changing moment. It was a cold winter night in a big city medical center. We had lived in that city for five months, but everyone we knew well enough to care about us still lived a long distance away. Nancy was facing thyroid surgery early the next morning for a growing nodule that was making simple swallowing a challenge. Facing surgery without close friends nearby raised our anxiety.

At that worrisome moment, Ralph chose to make an appearance. He was a colleague from work. I did not know Ralph well, but apparently he had heard about Nancy's surgery and made a special trip to the hospital to bring a listening ear and some well-wishes. Ralph had a ready smile and a gentle demeanor. He helped to distract us from our worries about the unknown. Would the finding be malignant? Would Nancy be facing radiation or chemotherapy? Would she lose her voice? Could we pay our bills if she could no longer work and we lost her paycheck from our family budget?

Ralph, however, shifted our attention to other topics. He asked us about our lives, our faith, our education, our families. When we did not expect it, Ralph asked if it would be all right if he prayed with us. We agreed while feeling a bit awkward, until Ralph asked to hold our hands and proceeded to lift Nancy, me, and our shared anxiety before God's throne of grace in a powerful prayer for successful surgery and God's intervention.

Ralph's prayer was a God incident for us. It felt like a switch had been flipped, and the Holy Spirit washed over us like a divine current of peace. Our anxious worries flowed away that night during Ralph's prayer, and I learned a valuable lesson. There are moments when we are most able to receive the blessing of the Holy Spirit. For many, immediately before surgery is one of those moments. Thanks are due to Ralph, for in my ministry I have made it a priority to try to be present with parishioners, family, and friends as an agent of Christ to offer to pray with them as they face medical procedures.

The Bible gives us additional directions for finding God. In the middle of a discussion about repairing relationships, Jesus says that if someone sins against us, we are to go to that person directly for a face-to-face meeting to try to work out our difficulties. Jesus offers us a solution to human arguments that is far less costly than war and more likely than a lawsuit to result in a positive outcome. But, if you have ever tried to take the advice of Jesus, you may know how difficult and messy such a face-to-face, sit-down meeting can be. Even with the best intentions, conflict resolution can be blocked by misunderstanding, deception, fatigue, and human pride. Conflicts can arise from a failure to recognize that the problem is merely a result of accumulating, but still hidden, pressures from elsewhere in the other person's life. Repairing relationships can be thwarted by miscommunication, or by the fact that your interests and mine may not be compatible. Families victimized by gun violence may never agree on gun legislation with those who make their living selling guns. Persons who believe in promoting positive family values will never be comfortable with drug dealers or pornographers in their neighborhoods.

Yet, it is in this uncomfortable and often dangerous middle ground of meeting face to face with our problem relationships that God incidents are likely to occur. Jesus promised to be present in that situation where faithful people risk themselves in efforts for reconciliation. In the middle of Christ's instructions about repairing relationships with our neighbors, Jesus declares in Matthew 18:20, "For where two or three are gathered in my name, there I am in the midst of them." Jesus emphasizes the importance of solving our disagreements peacefully.

If we want to be right with God and in this place of reconciliation where Jesus said He would be present, He highlights this command of working out our problems with others. In Matthew 5:23 He lets us know that living in right relationship with each other is more important than an offering given to God at the altar; furthermore, it takes first place. When Jesus teaches His followers to pray, He links our forgiveness of others with God's forgiveness of our offenses: "Forgive us our debts, as we also have forgiven our debtors" (Matthew 5:12).

Another place in the Bible that Jesus indicates that He will be present is in neighborhoods where love is being shared with the poor. In a community where I served in ministry, the local real estate ads regularly included this line: "Good, west location." The town was divided east and west by a river that clearly defined two worlds. The older, east side of town featured tired houses, broken families, lower incomes, higher unemployment, greater social needs, and nearly 100 percent of the town's minority population. All of the town's major investments in improvements for the prior 20 years had taken place on the west side of the river. People living on the west side may have felt that God blessed them with good schools, green lawns, safe streets, and newer homes. Churches built west of the river were more likely to feature such amenities as air-conditioning in the sanctuary and stainless steel kitchens. Thus, one might try to make a biblical case that God is more interested in life on the west side. After all, it regularly happens that persons who have won the lottery, or who prevail in sports, or who prosper in business, publicly express gratitude to God for their blessing.

However, the Bible declares God's primary concern for the poor. In Psalm 139, David expressed the truth that there is no place that God is not already present. God is especially to be found in those neighborhoods where faithful people are working to improve the lot of the poor. In one of Jesus' most important stories, the Last Judgment (Matthew 25), the nations of the world are gathered before the king. The ruler of the universe sends favorite servants to a place of eternal reward and sentences the disobedient to be condemned. Separating the saved from the condemned is a measure of the human heart. The rewarded fed the hungry, welcomed the stranger, gave drink to the thirsty, clothed the naked, and visited the sick and imprisoned. In summary, the King declared, "As you have done it to the least of these my brothers and sisters, you have done it unto me."

It is not difficult to find the "east side of the river" anywhere in the world. One in seven persons on earth today is living in hunger. Most American prisons are filled to capacity. Nearly half the children in America are being born out of wedlock. Single mothers and their children are more likely to live in poverty. The opportunities to serve Christ and meet God in care for the poor are near to all.

The Bible indicates that we can expect to experience God incidents in our efforts to forgive and reconcile with others. We can encounter God in our work with the least of God's children; we may also expect to encounter God when we are fulfilling the mission that Christ gave to His disciples. At the end of Matthew's Gospel (chapter 28), Jesus gives His disciples a job description: be busy making disciples worldwide through baptism and following his commandments. This work of disciple making is accompanied by a promise that indicates God incidents are sure to follow. Jesus said, "Lo, I am with you always, to the close of the age."

In John's Gospel (chapter 14), Jesus reinforces the idea that His living presence with us is linked to following His commandments. While Jesus was meeting with His closest friends in an upper room before his crucifixion, He taught them to keep His commandments as an expression of their love for Him. In return He promised to send the Holy Spirit to live within them. A key to seeing God at work in our lives is to spend our time living faithfully in those neighborhoods where Jesus taught us that God can surely be found. Experiencing God incidents is more likely for those who keep God's commandments and teach others to do the same.

It surprises many to learn that God is ever present precisely in those places in life where we are most likely to complain about God's absence. The Psalmist David noted that God was present "when I walk through the valley of the shadow of death, I will fear no evil because you are with me." Psalm 34 declares, "God is near to the brokenhearted and saves the crushed in spirit." This great source of comfort has been confirmed in multiple settings: rescue missions, soup kitchens, prisons, and hospice houses. In these places it is not unusual to hear the sincere testimonials of persons whom the world would easily label as broken, but who, in their most difficult moments, have discovered a closer connection with God.

God is always present, but we can put ourselves closer to where God has promised to be. We are more likely to experience God incidents if we serve as God has commanded in places where the Bible and experience have taught us that He can be found.

CHAPTER 12

INCIDENTS

FLYING BLIND

IF YOU HAD to choose one core value to follow in your life what would it be and why?

A recurring theme in this book, because it is a recurring theme in life, is that there really are times when we are totally blind to what God is doing. Ken helped me with an important lesson for navigating through life's fog.

Ken is a pilot by profession, an engineer by academic training, and a proud veteran who cut his teeth in aviation by flying air transports for the U.S. Army and the Army Reserves. After retiring from the military, Ken slid into the captain's seat by flying jets for a major American airline. In his spare time, he built his own experimental aircraft.

I respect Ken's abilities and his attention to detail in the way he manages his life, so I quickly accepted his invitation to join him for a flight in his plane. After single-handedly pulling his lightweight fiberglass craft out of the airport hangar, he asked me to hand-crank the front wheel down. Ken's cozy plane looked somewhat like a canopied go-cart with wings. I was assigned the task of keeping my eye on the gas gauge, a small plexiglass window situated behind my seat, where I could turn to see if there was any fuel still sloshing in the tank. My flight with Ken was a grand adventure. The countryside was glorious from above, and Ken was every bit as accomplished a pilot as I imagined.

In midair I asked Ken: "What is the most difficult part of flying?"

He said: "The greatest challenge is flying in the clouds because your visibility disappears. Without the ability to see distant points for reference, it is easy to become completely disoriented. When you are flying blind in the clouds, it is almost impossible to tell important things like speed, altitude, and direction."

"How do you fly in the clouds without crashing?" I asked.

Ken said: "You have to learn to trust your instruments. When your visuals are absent, and your body is unable to tell you if you are flying right-side up or upside down, your instruments will show you where you are, and where you are going."

Ken's wisdom about trusting your instruments when you are flying in the clouds has direct application to life. There are moments when storms come, clouds thicken, and we can lose our way. It is precisely in those moments of decreased visibility when we need to trust God, keep His commandments, and hold to the disciplines of our faith. It is easy to abandon faith when flying through the clouds, with terrible consequence.

Don is another person who, more than most, knows about flying blind in faith. Don is a counselor who specializes in working with sex offenders. Don shared his dramatic testimony in church and spoke of the day his daughter was gang-raped. The congregation listened in stunned silence. Don shared how the rapists unknowingly showed up at his office for counseling, driving his daughter's stolen car. The audience that morning identified with the truth that there are horrible moments in life when neither God's presence, nor God's will, are neither seen nor felt. Real life can cloud our vision of God. Don related how he was able to make it through the session only by keeping his focus on his training as a

counselor and his belief in a loving God. He confessed that
the rage within him would otherwise have been blinding. Don
helped us all when he related what he did with his rage. He
had a debriefing session with a colleague. He spent time with
God in prayer where he was honest about his rage. He let the
authorities handling his daughter's case administer justice.

I have witnessed on many occasions with deep sadness
how people of vital faith have gotten disoriented in the
clouds of life and have lost their way. It is tragic when couples
whose marriages are in trouble drop out of involvement in a
supportive church community. Many who find themselves
in financial difficulty forget stewardship principles and turn
instead to the lure of gambling as a solution to their problems.
It is not unusual for people overwhelmed by stress at work
to compound their problems by turning to alcohol or drugs
rather than to God in prayer or to trusted spiritual counselors.

If we apply a pilot's wisdom about flying through the
clouds to our experience of living, it is especially when the
God of goodness seems absent that we need to trust the
instruments of faith. There are habits of a faithful life that
are worth relying on when we are otherwise lost. Keep God's
great commandments. Focus on the love of God. Stay steady
in prayer. Study the Bible. Invest your treasure in God's work.
Exercise compassion. Keep close to supportive friends. Seek
wise counsel from others whose advice you trust. Follow Jesus'
teachings.

Proverbs 3:5-6 offers additional guidance especially for
moments when the presence of God feels invisible in life's
cloudy moments:

> "Trust in the LORD with all your heart, and do not
> rely on your own insight. In all your ways acknowl-
> edge him, and he will make straight your paths."

While in prayer in the Garden of Gethsemane, in a cloudy
moment, Jesus agonized over the trials He knew were coming.
Luke 22 tells us He was in such distress that in the midst of
prayer His sweat became like great drops of blood falling

upon the ground. Jesus pleaded with God, "Father if Thou art willing, remove this cup from Me." Even though Jesus knew that a horrible death by crucifixion was coming, He still had the discipline to trust His faith in God when He prayed, "Nevertheless, not My will but Thine be done."

It is easy to lose our way when flying through the clouds. We have witnessed the ending of healthy marriages, the destruction of once vital careers, and the crashing of upstanding citizens who have made immoral choices. Often these tragic events were preceded by a period of fog, like the death of a loved one, or a bad turn in business that shook faith at its foundations.

God incidents that can encourage faith may not be as readily seen when your life is surrounded by dense fog. There are times in life when it is important, like a pilot in the fog, to trust our instruments, which for believers are the lessons learned from scripture, the examples of the saints, and the consistent desire to honor God in all things.

CHAPTER 13

GOD INCIDENTS

ARE ENOUGH

WHOM DO YOU admire for their courage?

Your life at the moment may read like a horror story. There is no doubt that painful memories can leave disfiguring scars on a person's spirit. Post-traumatic stress is not a condition we can wish away. It is also true that powerful memories of God incidents can sustain belief even in the midst of a horrible present.

Mabel was smiling. How was that possible? Mabel's husband had left her 20 years earlier for another woman and she had lived alone and struggled financially ever since. Her daughter had just had a double mastectomy as a result of breast cancer. Mabel was living frugally on Social Security disability. Her savings were nonexistent, and her furnace had just died in the middle of a brutal winter. She was still recuperating from hip-replacement surgery, and her arthritis was acting up.

"Mabel, are you on drugs?" I asked.

"No, why would you think that?"

"You have just shared with me your history. If I were you, I would be thinking about screaming at God or making a date with severe depression. Yet, here you are with a smile that won't quit, and, outwardly, you don't even appear to be troubled. How do you do it?"

Mabel's reply taught me something important about God incidents.

She said "I know God exists. I have had experiences with God that are stored permanently in my heart. I remember the campfire at summer camp when I answered the call from a visiting evangelist and walked forward to accept Jesus as my Lord and Savior. I was overcome with the Holy Spirit and felt embraced by the loving presence of God. I also remember the time when my daughter was sick with pneumonia, and we didn't know if she would live. After I spent an evening praying with her and for her, her fever broke and she recovered. I know that God was present then.

"I remember the great joy of falling in love. I will not forget the awesomeness of God in my first trip to the Rocky Mountains. There are so many memories I can point to. I know in my heart that God was with me then, so when I come to places in my life like now, where the presence and the love of God are harder to see, I can continue to trust in God. Even if I never experience another moment of God's peace, all I need to do is remember how God has been present with me in the past, and that memory is enough."

Mabel taught me what people of faith have known for a long time. God incidents are gifts that keep on giving. Our memories of the past activity of God in our lives can help counter adversity with courage and hope. Christians sing hymns that recall God's actions, and we teach stories of past events to remind ourselves of God's goodness. Again and again, the Bible tells of God's mighty acts, such as the freeing of the Hebrew people from slavery in Egypt and caring for them for 40 years in the wilderness. Memories of God's actions are built into the annual seasons of our faith. We remember in worship God's mighty acts of the past so we may believe in God's leadership in the present and the future. The Bible is full of role models who are able to understand that life has its challenges but choose to believe in God anyway. The God incidents that we remember give us the ability to keep on loving God, even at times when evidence of God's love is harder to see.

There are many biblical characters who chose to believe in God even in the middle of great difficulty. These are God incidents where they were surprised to find God still at work.

Take King David. He began his life as a shepherd boy in Bethlehem tending his father's flocks. He then became well-known by defeating Goliath with his slingshot. David's fame spread with the words of his songs found in the book of Psalms. Psalm 34 recalls one of the darkest periods of David's life. When jealous King Saul put a price on his head, David looked for help from Abimelech, a neighboring king, and discovered that Abimelech also wanted him dead. David fled to the wilderness. While hiding in a cave he wrote, "I will bless the Lord at all times. His praise shall continually be in my mouth." Like Mabel, David's ability to praise God in tough times was grounded in a faith that remembered how God had been present in his past and trusted that God would be there in the future. David also wrote of God in Psalm 23, "Though I walk through the valley of the shadow of death, I will fear no evil, for Thou art with me, Thy rod and Thy staff, they comfort me."

Another biblical God incident occurred in the life of a character who boldly chose belief in God even when there seemed to be overwhelming evidence of evil all around him. Mighty enemies were moving against God's people and Habakkuk was an old man. His bones were deteriorating and his balance was tottering. The crops were failing in his farming community. Still, Habakkuk voiced his undying faith in God and promised to rely on the Lord for strength (Habakkuk 3:16-19).

Mabel, David, and Habakkuk are not the only persons who have decided to keep trusting in God when their lives became difficult. The Apostle Paul had a life full of God incidents that inspired his faith. Acts 9 and Galatians tell of the dramatic God incident that led to Paul's belief in Jesus and his life of missionary service. Later, while awaiting execution in Rome, Paul wrote a letter of love to his close friends in the church at Philippi in Macedonia. Still faithful, he encouraged his friends to rejoice, to have no worry, and to tell God thankfully of their requests. He believed that the peace of God would keep our hearts and minds in Christ no matter what might occur (Philippians 4:4-7).

Even Jesus, a man Christians worship as the very embodiment of God, chose faith while dying on a Roman cross. Both Matthew and Mark remembered Jesus crying from the cross: "My God, my God, why have You forsaken Me."[18]

In his book, *The Last Words of Christ*, author Adam Hamilton notes that Jesus was reciting the first words of Psalm 22 in much the same way we might draw upon memories in a time of testing to sing a line from a familiar hymn: "Amazing Grace, how sweet the sound that saved a wretch like me." Psalm 22 begins by describing a desperate human condition but ends with a great statement of faith: "All the ends of the earth shall remember and turn to the Lord; and all the families of the nations shall worship before Him" (Psalm 22:27). If Jesus could praise God while hanging on a cross, surely we can believe that there is no human circumstance where we can be separated from God's eternal love for us.

Mabel and others like her are living reminders that we are each central players in how the events around us are perceived. Do we recognize God's presence and find reason to praise God even in bad times? Or do we complain and allow our faith to slip away? That is a personal decision each of us must make.

When, as a new pastor, I wrestled with one of life's most important questions: "Where is God in our pain?" I wrote this poem that gives voice to my conviction that God incidents are found even in the midst of difficult and painful circumstance:

_____

18 Matthew 27:46; Mark 15:34.

Where is God When It Rains

When the doctor says, "I'm sorry,"
And the bill is stamped, "PAST DUE";
Or you turn to friends in search of hope
And there is nothing they can do.
When parents fade before your eyes
And children run away,
When dreams are dashed, no reason why,
No matter what you pray.
Where is God when it rains?
When adultery becomes a name
And "drugs" move in next door,
When morning dawns upon your shame
And evening falls with more.
When truth is covered by excuse
And grudge infects for years.
When walls of hell have broken loose,
Substantiating fears.
Where is God when it rains?
When dreams and other fantasies
Tax away your dime.
When headlines are a nightmare
And help is wasting time.
When the verdict is read in your name
And the penalty is due.
When the road is steep and rocky
And the place of rest is, too.
Where is God when it rains?
When life drenches us with raindrops, it also showers pain.
Who can see a rainbow when blinded by the rain?
Who can live through drowning and ever understand

When buffeted by storms for which no one ever planned?
Perhaps the rain is falling for the flower in the seed.
Perhaps it is a reminder to meet our neighbor's need.
Because the rain provokes us to plea the question "Why?"
Perhaps it leads us to the one that reigns o'er you and I.
I have seen God in the heavens and know there is more than me.
I know God by the faithful who care for the "least of these."
God has come in person in those who hurt like me.
That is why I keep on loving Him when raindrops fall on me.
I've felt God in the presence of an understanding friend,
And I've seen the Lord in scripture with its promise for the end.
I know that Christ has died for us and that is another reason why
I can keep on loving God when rain falls from the sky.
Have you seen God in the sunshine, in the light of answered prayer?
Have you known God in the victory of providential care?
Remember, heaven's wisdom also worked upon the eye
That tears may drop and love may grow when rain falls from the sky.

CHAPTER 14

GOD INCIDENTS

WHILE STANDING ON
HOLY GROUND

HAVE YOU EVER stood on holy ground?

"Moses, take off your shoes. You are standing on holy ground" (Exodus 3:5).

There are times and places where we are especially aware that we are in the presence of the holy and are filled with a sense of awe. These holy-place God incidents are often life-changers. Many look for ways to hold onto these moments and to extend them. Some of the world's holiest temples have been built on the exact location where a remembered God incident occurred.

Have you ever experienced a holy ground moment where you became aware of the presence of God? An orderly in a major medical center helped me to realize that holy ground experiences are not just stories in the Bible. The orderly had pushed a parishioner in a hospital bed on the way to open heart surgery, stopping before the swinging doors that were clearly marked in bold letters: "Surgical Suite. Authorized Personnel Only Beyond This Point."

The sick man's family gathered around his bed.

The orderly said: "This is where we part company. Give dad your hugs and kisses and final prayers here. I'll give you all a minute before I take him into surgery."

The orderly turned to me with a knowing smile and whispered: "I call this place, 'Amen Corner.' This is holy ground we're standing on, you know. Of all the places in the hospital, I know God is here."

Suddenly, I was struck by the sacred nature of the drama playing out in front of me. Hopes, fears, tears, and love made that space and time holy. Each person wanted the precious goodbyes to last. Heartfelt prayers were offered to God. A place I had visited many times before had been given holy meaning. I no longer see that space as just another hallway. In my pastoral role, it is a place I visit often to walk with families and their loved ones on the way to surgery. Now, I expect to experience God's presence there. "Amen Corner" at the hospital is holy ground.

That hospital orderly helped me to think of other sacred places where God incidents are more likely to happen. I experienced a holy encounter with God in the wedding of our daughter, Bethany, which began with the ceremonial procession of the bridal party into the church. The climax of the entrance was the walk of the bride, my daughter, adorned in her specially chosen dress and accompanied by me. The bridal march ended with a statement by the pastor, followed by a powerful pause and a life-changing handoff as the pastor asked: "Who presents this woman to be married to this man?"

In the seconds that followed, this dad remembered his years with his daughter and powerful memories came flooding back. I was aware in that moment that life was about to change forever as I spoke words that entrusted our treasured daughter to the care of a new son-in-law. In a moment only a parent can fully understand, the words were spoken, "Her mother and I do." Heaven came near.

These moments of heightened awareness of God can catch us by surprise. Such was the case during my first visit to St. Peter's Basilica, the mother church for Roman Catholicism. When I first saw the Pieta, the priceless sculpture by Michelangelo of Mary holding the lifeless body of the crucified Christ across her lap, I was overcome by its beauty. The prayers of over a billion Christians focus on this place. The basilica was built over the grave of the Apostle Peter who, because of his love for Jesus, had been crucified there, upside down. I suddenly felt the warm embrace of God's love. Tears of joy spontaneously flowed. God's love filled that space.

Not only in great cathedrals do holy ground moments occur. A meeting with the holy can come in humble settings as well. On a tour of the Temple of Luxor, along the banks of the Nile River south of Cairo, a 10-year-old Egyptian child followed a group of Americans through the temple. The barefoot boy, wearing the simple clothing of a peasant, spoke only Arabic. The guide translated his persistent invitation for the Americans to join him at his house for tea after their tour. When the invitation was accepted, Jamal beamed.

Jamal's nearby residence was a mud hovel built just outside the temple on a small hill. The only entrance was an open doorway. Everyone stooped low to enter and sat to keep from hitting heads on the dirt ceiling. On the dirt floor was a worn wooden bed frame with ropes laced across the opening like a hammock. There was no electricity, no visible plumbing, no interior decorating, no windows, just the bed. An unlikely rainstorm would have melted the structure into a puddle of mud. The visitors crouched and gingerly sat on the edge of the wooden bed frame. Jamal built a small fire of gathered twigs, scooped the drying and previously used tea leaves off his front stoop and into a weathered metal pot that contained water he had pumped at the temple.

The guests asked Jamal about his life. The guide, acting as interpreter, revealed that Jamal was an orphan. His mother had died during his delivery. His father, a soldier in the Egyptian Army, had been killed in a recent war. His uncle had arranged for the mud hovel and for the steady job for Jamal.

Jamal kept an eye on the temple after hours to prevent looting and to report trespassing.

When the tea was brewed, this gentle child poured it into the single china cup that he owned and passed the cup to his guests, urging each to sip in turn. It was a moment of Holy Communion like none other. The sharing of Jamal's cup of tea was a God incident of deep significance. When persons who have nothing freely offer everything they have, their gift can change the recipient. A space labeled "generous hospitality for strangers" had been created by God, Who made a hovel holy and touched a group of friends through Jamal.

God incidents on holy ground can occur anywhere. It could be at a loved one's grave, or at the scene of an accident where life was spared. We may encounter God during a walk in the forest, or in the company of a child enchanted by a butterfly dancing in a spring meadow. The psalmist declares in Psalm 139 that there is nowhere we can go to flee from God's presence. In Romans, Paul wrote, "Nothing can separate us from the love of God." Holy ground moments can spark a relationship with our Creator. They can change beliefs about life's ultimate purpose and inspire us to rearrange our priorities.

CHAPTER 15

GODINCIDENTS

IN

GREAT CONFLICT

DO YOU BELIEVE that God can work through conflict?

I believe that many persons are driven from faith by conflict. Examine fractured families, failing companies, dying churches, and disbelieving persons; the odds are good you will find unresolved conflict in each case.

Should you ask where to go to find a living faith in God, I would be tempted to take you to church camp on a clear summer evening by a picturesque lake as the campfire crackles and the stars twinkle in the sky. We would sit with good friends, loving the moment, holding hands, and singing "Kum ba yah" in perfect harmony. Many persons point to inspiring God incidents like this when they recount their first intentional decision to follow Jesus. God incidents often are remembered with adjectives such as "warm," "loving," "intimate," and "spiritual." Because loving God and neighbor are the two greatest commandments, it is likely to assume that God would be most visible in neighborhoods where love is strongest. I have no doubt that God does shape faith in such moments. Many persons find this love while serving as volunteers in soup kitchens, homeless shelters, residential hospice facilities, and the like.

God is present not only when love is clearly evident in the happy moments of life. God's presence also is identified in the middle of great conflict, though we may need time and distance after a skirmish to recognize and fully appreciate God's design. Knowing how God is able to help us work through disagreements can help us to stay faithful when we are in the middle of the battle.

Conflict is defined as a disagreement, a difference of opinion, a battle, or a prolonged struggle. As old as history and as current as the evening news, conflict can be the motivation to maintain a strong military, prisons, and police. Energy in conflict, like a flame on a candle, has potential for good or for destruction. That flame can light a room or cook a meal. That same fire is also capable of destroying a building. Similarly, conflict has within it potential for pain or for healing. Conflict not only can lead us to doubt God's existence, but also can reveal God's goodness. Conflict can create bitter enemies, but it is equally capable of forging the deepest friendships.

Just as a pearl forms in the oyster as a result of the irritation caused by a grain of sand, with the passage of time we can recognize how unrest reveals God's glory. One such life-shaping conflict began in 1517 A.D. between Martin Luther, a German Catholic monk, and Johann Tetzel, a Roman Catholic indulgence salesman. Tetzel was working for both the Roman Catholic pope, Leo X, as well as the local bishop, inviting the people of Wittenburg, Germany, to buy special certificates, called indulgences, on behalf of their loved ones. The church promised that these certificates would hasten entrance into heaven. This implied that most people at death were not bad enough for hell nor yet good enough for heaven, and could make it over the hump with a little financial help from family and friends. Luther, a faculty member in religion at the university in Wittenberg, protested the practice of selling indulgences because he found no biblical reasons for buying forgiveness from God. He argued instead that our salvation is promised by the full and sufficient sacrifice of Jesus on the cross and is a free gift of God's grace.

The conflict over the selling of indulgences sparked a reform movement in the church that gave rise to new branches of Christianity. This Protestant Reformation was inspired by the idea that the Bible, even more than the pope, should be the primary authority in guiding Christian living. The conflict between Catholics and Protestants has helped extend God's love in new directions.

History gives us a similar view on other conflicts which have led to major change. Abraham Lincoln, Mahatma Gandhi, Martin Luther King Jr., and Nelson Mandela are well known historical figures who engaged in great struggles for justice. Slaves who are now free, and other persons around the world who have directly benefited from expanded civil rights, acknowledge God's hand working through these struggles.

Ordinary people also can experience the presence of God in the middle of conflict. Energy in conflict, harnessed and guided, can stimulate new growth. It is not unusual for soldiers who have been to war to form lifelong bonds of deepest friendship with comrades in arms. In sports, it is common to find bitter rivals forming lasting relationships after their playing days are over.

On a more personal level is a God incident in my own family's history, where conflict resulted in evidence of God's involvement. George Maris, my earliest known American ancestor, was a Quaker who came to this country with William Penn in 1682 to help found the colony of Pennsylvania. He came to America after serving a prison sentence in England for the crime of worshipping God in his own home. That conflict strengthened George's passion for religious freedom. The subsequent impact of his offspring on American life is significant.[19]

---

19 A listing of some of George and Alice Maris's famous offspring can be found at the website www.maris.net/gen/famous.htm

It may be argued that life in America is somewhat different today because God worked through the conflict of an unjust imprisonment to inspire George Maris to leave England and settle in this new land.

Another personal God incident occurred during a family vacation in the Rocky Mountains when a surprise discovery taught me an unforgettable insight about God. During a nature hike in a national park, the ranger pointed out the charred devastation caused by a recent major forest fire. It seemed the destruction across several mountainsides contained only tragedy. I could imagine the horror that survivors feel when witnessing similar scenes following the devastations of war.

The ranger, however, surprised us. He told us forest fires are a necessary part of the life cycle of nature. Burning old trees away enables new life to flourish. It also provides room for meadows, which are needed to support life that is not possible when the forest is full and the undergrowth is dense. The park ranger pointed to a spot beneath the ash where we could glimpse the small green blossoming seeds that germinate only after the fire. The field that first seemed like nature's graveyard already was becoming nature's nursery. Without the ranger's educated eyes and quiet words, God's treasure would have remained unknown to us.

God incidents can be seen in the middle of, or long after, life's great conflicts. When your spirit is wounded, do not give up hope. God is still alive and active. In the Bible, the prophet Isaiah offers these words of hope to a people who have experienced devastation. This sage servant of God knows He is present even in the aftermath of destructive warfare: "Those who wait for the Lord shall renew their strength, they shall mount up with wings like eagles, they shall run and not be weary, they shall walk and not faint" (Isaiah 40:31).

CHAPTER 16

INCIDENTS

IN THE RUNNING

CONVERSATION

CAN PEOPLE BE used as instruments for the delivery of
God's message?

In religious pulpits all across the world, people regularly
deliver sermons in which they proclaim that they are speaking
on God's behalf and delivering God's authoritative word. It
is no secret that many of these messengers give God a bad
name. In some cases the words of the preacher are fouled
by ignorance or bigotry. Sometimes the words are nullified
because the preacher articulates one message and lives another.
If you have been disillusioned and scarred by words delivered
in God's name, I am truly sorry. I would encourage you not
to give up on God because of the faults of the messengers.
I urge you to keep listening with an open mind for God's
word, which, when delivered in love by a servant whose life
is aligned with God's grace, has the capacity to change life for
the good.

The Bible offers this important insight about God incidents.
God communicates with humanity and calls on us to serve as
agents for divine purposes. For all the high-profile instances
when people speaking in God's name get it wrong, people are

also capable of serving as positive representatives of God's love and grace.

It is possible for us to hear and answer God's commands. Some never get the message. Some choose to ignore it. Others refuse to believe that such messages are possible, or they clearly understand what God is asking but feel the task is too difficult and the outcome doubtful. God's commands for us are in the best interests of humanity, but they can conflict with cultural, popular, or commercial interests. If growing a world where peace, love, and personal fulfillment are desired goals, can we make sense of the great wealth squandered on flourishing businesses which undermine these objectives?

Because humanity has a demonstrated ability to ignore, reject, or forget God's desires, the Bible teaches that some are called to the challenging task of communicating God's word to the people. John the Baptist was inspired to tell an adulterous King Herod to repent (Matthew 14:8). In the book of Jonah God commanded His prophet Jonah to deliver a message to the Assyrian enemies in Nineveh, ordering them to turn away from their evil ways. God gave Isaiah the unsavory assignment to preach to a people who would neither hear, nor heed, him (Isaiah 6). Samuel fared no better. God called him to be His voice and to utter God's judgment on Samuel's friend and mentor, Eli and his family (1 Samuel 3:18). Further, in John's Gospel, the risen Jesus gave Peter a forewarning that the day would come when Peter would be compelled to go where he did not wish to go (John 21).

God's agents are not always eloquent, nor eager to begin God's work. Moses tried to beg off from serving as God's prophet in the court of the Pharaoh of Egypt by claiming he was slow of speech (Exodus 4). Jeremiah asked whether he was old enough to serve as God's messenger (Jeremiah 1:6). Zechariah was more than reluctant when he was ordered to proclaim to the people gathered in the Temple that his infertile wife would soon be pregnant (Luke 1).

The Bible tells us that when God speaks, life happens. In the eloquent description of creation in Genesis 1, it is the word of God that brings life into being. In John's Gospel, the apostle begins his purposeful recounting of Jesus' life and ministry with the assertion that God's word is the source of our life and our hope (John 1:1-5).

In his letter to the Romans, the Apostle Paul noted that God chooses some to speak on His behalf, and argued that without these servants it would be difficult for people to believe in a God they had never known (Romans 10).

The Bible tells that people came to hear Jesus preach because He spoke the word of God (Luke 5). Following the death and ascension of Jesus, His followers carried on with the important task of delivering God's word to the world. Acts 4:31 records those preaching moments in this way: "And when they had prayed, the place in which they were gathered together was shaken; and they were all filled with the Holy Spirit and spoke the word of God with boldness."

These Biblical memories remind us that God incidents also happen during the preaching event. Persons often say their decision to follow Jesus occurred after hearing the words of a believer preaching, teaching, or witnessing on God's behalf.

Jesus reminds us that the act of sharing our faith is God-inspired. He warns His disciples that the day will come when they will be asked to defend their faith in court. But He tells them not to worry, for the Holy Spirit will provide the necessary words in that hour (Luke 12).

Many holy places demonstrate the importance of the sermon with raised pulpits and focused lighting. Clergy vestments, seminary training, and ordination ceremonies remind us that we can hear about God through a preacher. The book of Acts tells an important God incident: After hearing Simon Peter preach, about 3,000 persons became followers of Jesus.

Weekly sermon preparation has taught me that God is often present in the work of getting ready. God incidents are an ongoing part of sermon preparation, delivery, and response. For me, sermons grow from an ongoing daily conversation with God that includes prayer, Bible study, dreaming, real-life encounters in the parish, reading, and paying attention to the daily news. A sermon, much like a fruit tree, somehow comes from the seed. The preacher plants the seed, waters, and weeds. It is God who brings the seed to fruition.

I once was invited to return for a congregational anniversary celebration to the pulpit of a church I had served 25 years before. Curious to know what people remembered from my earlier years of preaching, I asked friends to share their memories. God gave me an important lesson. No one remembered my ease in sharing the latest insights from well-known theologians. No one remembered my ability to quote the right chapter and verse of scripture, nor my words of prophetic challenge. However, they did remember that I had conducted the funeral for their father or that I had prayed with them in the hospital before surgery. They remembered that I had officiated at their wedding or baptized their babies, that they were bald like me, and that I fell off a roof and fractured my spine. The human elements of our lives during our time together were the words of God which were remembered and which strengthened the bonds of love that endured over time. The relationship between a pastor and congregation which grows by sharing life can make it more likely that the words of the preacher are remembered by the hearer.

It is important to note that often a word which changes the life of another is a God incident delivered by an ordinary human being in the course of normal conversation. The word can come by way of a reprimand: "Did you know that name-calling is not helpful?" God can speak when a respected teacher asks: "What do you want to be when you grow up? Have you ever thought about a career helping others?" The word of God can come by way of encouragement: "You have a real gift for that." The word can be delivered by way of an invitation: "Do you have a church home? Would you like to worship with us on Sunday?" In looking back over the journey we have traveled, it is often the inspired word of ordinary people that makes a significant difference in the road we choose to travel.

It is also true that words which inspire, encourage, and heal are also capable of perverting, tempting, discouraging, and inciting others. The Apostle Paul noted in one of his letters to the Corinthian church that "we have this treasure in earthen vessels." (2 Corinthians 4:7). Paul wanted his friends to know that the word he proclaimed was from God and not himself. But we need to acknowledge the earthen vessels that deliver this word are often flawed. When our actions fail to line up with the words we profess Paul also noted, "Though I speak with the tongues of men and of angels but have not love, I am a noisy gong or a clanging cymbal." (1 Corinthians 13:1).

Again, if you have been disillusioned and scarred by words you will never forget, delivered by a hypocrite acting in God's name, please know I am truly sorry. I can only urge you to keep listening for God's word. When God's word is delivered in love by a servant whose life is aligned with God's grace, God's word has the capacity to change life for the good.

The Bible reminds us, and life confirms, the word of the Lord offers occasions for God to speak to us if we are open to receive.

CHAPTER 17

SACRIFICE

GOD INCIDENTS

AND THE

SACRIFICIAL CALL

HAVE YOU EVER been asked to do something that you did not want to do?

Many of us wish that God incidents would confine themselves only to those things that that make us feel good. I am partial to memories where God does all the work, or where God invites me to accept tasks that are light, gentle, and warm. "Yes Lord, I will gladly love the children. You want me to take time off from work each week to rest? I can handle that. You would not like me to murder others? I will restrain myself when the urge comes." These are easy requests, and I willingly obey.

On the other hand, the Bible is very clear that God is also made known frequently in commands to do something that is sacrificial for Him. God is aware of the point where His commands are met by our contrary human willfulness. God's desires often run opposite to the popular, politically supported, and big-money business of human sin. In the role of commander-in-chief of the universe, God has called on humanity to do things that cause the faint of heart to buckle at the knees.

A memorable example of a God incident where the Almighty was made known in a sacrificial task is God calling Moses to lead the Israelites out of their slavery in Egypt. In Exodus we read about Moses, a simple man, minding his own business, tending his flock of sheep. Suddenly, Moses was staring at the unbelievable sight of a bush aflame but not burning up.

In that moment of wonder, God spoke to Moses. Based on the Biblical account, we can imagine God's conversation with Moses, asking him to do what appears to be impossible and sounding something like this: "Moses, I have a job for you. I want you to return to the country where you are still wanted for a murder you committed. Go to the Pharaoh, whose father ordered a nationwide manhunt for you. Meet with him. Tell him to free your people from slavery. Pharaoh will not voluntarily relinquish his control of slaves, who are the source of his wealth and political power. I must teach him that I am God and he is not. I will bring plagues upon the Egyptians. Pharaoh will punish my people by increasing their workload. You will be despised by many of those you are actually trying to help. Pharaoh will finally agree to let my people go when all Egyptian families suffer the death of their first born."

Moses flinched. Who wouldn't? Who wants to give up a safe job for a sacrificial mission with impossible odds? Moses asked for proof that this message truly was from God. He urged God to get someone else for the job. He couldn't speak well; he stuttered. But God did not change His mind.

The call of Moses is not the only biblical God incident where God commands someone to do a difficult job. God called Isaiah to serve Him as a prophet and outlined an impossible mission. In chapter 6 God orders Isaiah to deliver a message, warning him the people would refuse to listen. They would reject hope and refuse to repent of their sin. In these and other encounters, the Bible teaches us that a life of faithfulness is not always easy.

What person wants to experience rejection and ridicule by delivering a message to unresponsive listeners? Yet there is no mention that Isaiah hesitated in doing what God commanded in this challenging God incident.

Obedience to God sometimes runs contrary to our desires. The point of decision where we either obey or ignore God is always an important God incident. Such decision points can be seen in the Ten Commandments. God engraved these laws for living on stone tablets that were delivered to Moses on Mount Sinai for the people. These commandments are recorded in Exodus 20 and Deuteronomy 5. These are not options, or suggestions to be followed when they are convenient. Disciples are not empowered to modify or try to improve on them. A walk through the dangerous and uncomfortable land where these commandments were first received makes it clear that abiding by these laws was necessary for the future of a migrant people. Breaking commandments weakens the trust necessary for a community to survive. But it is human nature to look for exceptions and to excuse ourselves from laws that are meant to be binding.

The fourth commandment, "Remember the Sabbath day, to keep it holy," is an example of an important law that is often disregarded by people in our complex culture. God's command to remember the Sabbath is tied in the Bible to God's promise of land for His people. Keeping a Sabbath every seven days is a pattern established by God in the creation of the universe. Resting one day each week helps us remember how God freed His people from slavery. Slaves don't get a day off from bondage. Sabbath is God's gift and a blessed reminder of our freedom. Sabbath-keeping is also linked to the ordering of God's creation. In the Genesis Chapter 1 account of creation, a pattern is established where each day begins in the evening. Humanity is not created until the sixth day of creation and then God rests on the seventh day as a weekly reminder that God is in charge of life, which continues even when we are asleep. In today's world, the biblical command, resting one day in seven, is shown to be healthy for the human body. Sharing in worship each week helps to strengthen community.

Choosing to order life in a weekly rhythm that remembers to put God first makes sense. But the obstacles to keeping the Sabbath day holy are many. Many are employed in necessary jobs which require working on the Sabbath. Others simply find excuses for ignoring this simple command of God because it seems easier than obeying. Different faith traditions choose different days to observe as Sabbath. However, the point is not which day is observed. What is important is the weekly choice to either obey God or ignore the commandment.

The Sabbath regularly gets pushed aside by families for the sake of sports, as coaches find it easier to schedule tournaments and practices when school is not in session. Many business people find it more profitable to cater to their customers seven days a week than to honor God by shuttering for a day each week as an expression of faith. The Sabbath gets ignored by many in favor of other pursuits.

Each decision to obey or ignore any of God's primary commandments is a God incident. There are observable consequences over time that come from disregarding God's commandments and removing God from consideration when making decisions. Cities that lack strong faith communities often are plagued by higher numbers of broken marriages, abused children, violent crime, addictive behaviors, and rising popularity of businesses such as gambling, drugs, human trafficking, and pornography.

When people choose to obey God's commands, life and community produce different results. When faith communities flourish, education is valued, strong families are encouraged, children are loved, support systems are developed, a climate of trust is established. A helpful way to confirm this conviction for yourself is to spend some time with the website www.neighborhoodscout.com. This website allows you to evaluate any neighborhood in the United States, evaluating current crime statistics against a national standard. You can confirm for yourself that communities with strong religious traditions have lower crime rates than cities where economic depression has eroded churches and social structures.

Sacrificial commands from God are given to us all. Jesus commands each of us to "love your enemies and do good to those who hate you." (Luke 6:27). This commandment sounds so easy when it is uttered in a worship setting from the lips of a polished speaker. In reality, however, forgiving enemies and doing good to those who actually persecute us is far harder when the abstract concept has a real name attached to a specific hurtful action. Similarly, Jesus commands us to believe in God. Responding to the love and acceptance of Jesus in obedience to this command is simpler when the sun is shining and our business is profitable. Belief in a good God is more difficult when the diagnosis is cancer or when evil moves in next door.

Imagine how a God Who created the world and has sacrificed a Son for that world feels about the regular snubs of a people who are indifferent to God's commands. God's commandments, the foundation of our life in community, are regularly ridiculed in TV and movie plots that glorify faithless behaviors.

Libby helped me to see God's hand in a sacrificial command. Following the death of her husband, Larry, a retired pastor, Libby came to me and presented a gift. "Larry wanted you to have this," she said. She handed me a beautiful piece of art, carved hands reaching toward each other like two friends in a clasped handshake. The hands, sculpted from a single block of wood, looked like the product of an African street artist.

Libby told this story about the hands: "In World War II, Larry was wounded in the Battle of the Bulge. A sniper's bullet hit him in his chest. Following the surgery that saved his life, the surgeon said, 'Larry, someone upstairs must be looking out for you. Your aorta was constricted when the bullet passed through your body. In another half a heartbeat, it would have been expanded with blood, the bullet would have nicked the vessel, and you would have bled out on the battlefield.'

"When Larry returned home from the war, he lived with an inescapable sense that God had spared him for a reason. We married, had four children, and Larry went to work for the U.S. Postal Service as a mail carrier. But God would not let Larry go. Larry felt called to ministry, so he gave up his secure income, and we all packed up and moved through seven years of college and ministry training.

"Larry's first ministry appointment was to a church in the Deep South during the tumult of the civil rights movement. Larry's all-white congregation had one major test question for their new pastor: 'If a black man comes through those doors, pastor, what will you do?'

"Without hesitation, Larry replied, 'I will do what Jesus desires; I will welcome him to our congregation and offer him my seat.'

"It was the right answer from a biblical perspective, but the wrong answer for the culture of Larry's first church. The congregation put up such a stink with the bishop's office that we were forced to move to a different church.

"During this turmoil, Larry heard about a man on the other side of the world who was also enduring persecution for his belief – the conviction that all people are equally loved by God. Larry began a correspondence with him. Who was the man? Bishop Desmond Tutu from South Africa. He was awarded the Nobel Peace Prize for his opposition to the South African policy of apartheid, and for his work to bring reconciliation to a broken nation. Grateful for their friendship, Bishop Tutu sent these carved hands to Larry."

The hands from one pastor to another were clasped in friendship that seemed to span both sea and time. In that moment of hearing Larry's story and receiving the gift from his widow, those hands were transformed for me into a treasure beyond measure, a remembered God incident that still inspires many who hear the story.

God incidents are not just in the miracle moments. As with Larry and Bishop Tutu, God often is made known in the difficult challenges of life when we are commanded to obey, and when obedience demands much of us.

CHAPTER 18

your dreams

GODINCIDENTS

MINING

DREAMS

WHAT CAN WE learn about ourselves and God from our dreams?

We have seen how God is made known in God incidents. We have learned about God from miracles and from times of great struggle. We have found that God is present in neighborhoods where Jesus told us to look for him. We experience God in the present and sometimes from the scenic lookout that enables us to see the long view behind and the road ahead. We understand how God can transform life in moments on holy ground and in the words of God given to us through others and which help shape our lives. God incidents can even occur in the content of our dreams.

Ira Progoff, an American psychotherapist and author, has written that our dreams are a rich source of information and can be inspirational for living. When we consciously remember our dreams after we awake, Progoff says, we can enrich our lives. He compares dream-awareness to a person lowering a pail into a deep well of the purest artesian water that flows in a never-ending stream. A remembered dream is like a bucket of that refreshing water brought to the surface.

Progoff suggests that our dreams are an important source of truth about us.[20]

The Bible tells us that for centuries dreams have been understood as one of the ways God communicates with humanity. Dreams are fertile soil for God incidents. The story of Joseph in the book of Genesis is one place in scripture where we are given a glimpse of how God works through dreams. Joseph was one of the youngest of a family which grew to include 12 sons. Because he was his father's favorite, Joseph was a target of family jealousy and sibling rivalry. When he boldly reports to his brothers his dreams that one day they will all bow down to his authority, the unfolding family drama (chapters 37-50) is more riveting than any reality television show. The biblical account reveals how God worked through Joseph's dream to protect a promise to these descendants of Abraham. The text implies that if there had been no dream, Joseph might never have been sold into slavery, and the unfolding faith story of the people of Israel would have had a very different plotline.

In the New Testament story about the conception of Jesus, we learn of another history-making dream from God. The engaged couple, Joseph and Mary, were the source of a scandal when it became known that Mary was pregnant outside of marriage, and Joseph was not the father. The Bible tells that an angel appeared to Joseph in a dream and told him what he was to do (Matthew 1:20-25). Joseph followed the advice of the angel and decided not to divorce Mary. If not for the God incident of the dream, Mary could have faced life as a single mother, and Christianity might not have occurred in the way we currently know it.

It is a fair question to ask: "How do we know that a dream is from God?" Counselors can readily testify that not all dreams have holy content. Persons who struggle with mental illness have dreams about harming themselves or others.

20 Ira Progoff, *At a Journal Workshop: Writing to Access the Power of the Unconscious and Evoke Creative Ability*, Penguin Books, 1992.

Others have dreams that are not fit for family conversation. Psychotherapists explain that dreams can be our subconscious way of processing feelings and emotions that accumulate in the course of living. Remembering our dreams and learning from them can be a helpful exercise in self-discovery.

It is more likely that a dream is from God if it is consistent with how God already has been revealed in the Bible. If a dream encourages violation of God's commandments or a public denial of Jesus, it may be good material for learning about ourselves but it should not be attributed to God.

Two of my dreams have led to the conviction that they are from God. My first life-changing dream occurred during my college years when I was growing into independence and adulthood. I was also meeting new people, especially girls. I began dating Nancy and discovered that I liked her. On the night of the dream, Nancy and I had driven to my parents' house to attend a concert in the city. At home after the concert, I fell asleep and had a clear vision that I was to marry Nancy. The next day I shared my great news with Nancy. My dream was her worst nightmare. She did not have the same impression of me. I was hurt. Why would God give me such a clear dream and then have that dream blow up in my face? Nancy began dating other people. I chose to study in another country.

Three years went by and I met Nancy again at a birthday party. We were married 10 months later. That dream-come-true has been a God incident and after 40 years is still a source of great happiness.

A second dream has offered deep guidance for me in ministry. In this dream I found myself in the middle of nowhere with herds of helpless sheep being drawn into a bottomless pit filled with black, gooey slime. The sides of the pit were scenes of a desperate struggle to escape by all who had fallen into it. I managed to free myself from the pit, but I felt helpless to rescue the thousands of sheep who were perishing. I resolved to use my freedom to prevent other sheep from dying in that pit. The solution, I believed, lay in the distant city visible on the far horizon. I journeyed toward the city to find a giant dredging machine to get rid of this hazard and save future sheep from this same fate.

The further I walked toward the city, the more my destination receded. Discouraged, I was met by a stranger on the road, who turned out to be Jesus. He asked where I was going. I explained to Him my close brush with death, my desire to save the sheep, and my plan to return to the pit with a dredging machine. Jesus asked: "In the meantime, how many sheep have you saved?"

"Jesus, my efforts will be more successful with a machine."

"Glenn, how many hands do you have? Couldn't you have saved even one?"

The dream freed me from thinking I have to save the world, but showed I can use my two hands to make a difference. I learned the decisions we make in the present moment are as important as our long-term plans. This dream of the sheep in the slimy pit has moved from my subconscious to a place in my life where it continues to help me make daily decisions. It is a God incident that reminds me that one of the ways we can experience God is through our dreams.

The New Testament book of Acts records how the Holy Spirit was poured out on Jesus' disciples at the Jewish Pentecost festival, 50 days after the Passover festival and the crucifixion of Jesus. This Holy Spirit event energized the followers of Jesus to share publicly their witness to a risen Lord. This history-changing God incident prompted the writer Luke to recall a passage of scripture where the prophet Joel anticipated this day happening. Joel wrote that God's spirit would be poured out on people, inspiring young men to see visions and old men to dream dreams (Acts 2:17 and Joel 2:28).

Persons have long believed that God can work through dreams. A statue, inspired by the dream of the prophet Isaiah, stands outside the United Nations building in New York City.

It encourages the world community to keep living toward God's dream of a day when we will beat our swords into plowshares (Isaiah 2:4). Another of Isaiah's dreams is the basis of artist Edward Hicks' masterpiece, "Peaceable Kingdom," which hangs in the National Gallery of Art in Washington, D.C. It depicts in oil paint an image of the day when the lion and the lamb will lie down together (Isaiah 11:6). The dreams of the Apostle John, recorded in the book of Revelation, are word pictures of God's triumphant future that continue to give believers hope for eternal life and a new creation. John Bunyan's classic book, *Pilgrim's Progress*, draws much of its material from John's dreams.

I believe that God continues to influence life through our dreams. Learning the content of God's dreams as recorded in the Bible and paying attention to our own sleeping visions can be a fruitful way for us to grow our relationship with God.

If you are having dreams you believe are from God but do not know what to make of them, you may want to share your dreams with trusted counselors like the boy Samuel did when he shared his visions with Eli the priest in 1 Samuel 3. Even King Belteshazzar sought help in understanding his dreams from Daniel in Daniel 2. Not all dreams come to pass. It can be a challenge to set the firm foundations of reality beneath the sand castles of our minds. Nonetheless, trust in this biblical wisdom: Dreams are fertile ground for God incidents.

CHAPTER 19

GOD INCIDENTS

THROUGH
PRAYER

WHAT IS YOUR experience of God through prayer?

Even though personal experience teaches us that not all prayers lead to positive results, prayer can be a God incident. When we are praying, God can draw near to us as we turn our thoughts toward Him. Persons who pray can be changed by the encounter.

My wife Nancy and I can point to our son, Michael, as dramatic evidence of the power of prayer to change lives. After struggling with infertility issues we prayerfully decided to begin our parenting through adoption. For two years we placed a box of Special K cereal on our kitchen table and prayed for our unknown and as yet unborn child from South Korea at every meal. Michael has now been a part of our family for thirty years. The evidence of God's answer to our prayers through this precious son is testament to the power of prayer far beyond our greatest dreams.

The Bible tells of many prayers that were God incidents. In Genesis 25, Isaac prayed to the Lord because his wife Rebekah was unable to conceive a child. We read of the happy God incident when Rebekah gave birth to twins, Jacob and Esau. Later, when King Solomon prayed for wisdom, his prayer was

answered directly by God (1 Kings 9). In 2 Kings 20, King
Hezekiah asked God for healing and the Bible relates his
prayers were answered. In the New Testament, the letter to
the Hebrews offers an encouraging word to those who value
prayer as a way to grow a relationship with God, "Let us then
with confidence draw near to the throne of grace, that we
may receive mercy and find grace to help in time of need"
(Hebrews 4). James, the brother of Jesus, also believed in the
power of prayer to connect us intimately with God. "Draw
near to God and He will draw near to you" (James 4:8).

But for all the positive discussion the Bible gives about
prayer, it is also true that unanswered prayers are often named
as the reason for disbelief. It is painful to turn to prayer and
ask God for help in a time of great trial and still to suffer loss.
We may understand our disappointment with God and with
prayer by looking at an analogy. Infomercials are designed to
sell products to consumers. They are offered for a limited time
and only through a prompt response to the 800 number on
the TV screen. Buyers tell how happy they are with the new
product. A polished sales rep proclaims for a low, low price in
just three easy payments you, too, can be satisfied. "But wait,
there's more!" A fabulous offer is made better when a bonus
is added for no extra charge if you buy the product within the
next 30 minutes. Many products sold in infomercials fail to
live up to their advertising.

We live in an age when persuasive televangelists have
promoted belief in the power of prayer with similarly exciting
promises. "If you only pray, you can tell your disease to be
gone, and you will be healed." Or, "If you only pray, you will
be successful, healthy, wealthy, and wise." Or, "If you pray,
then your prayers will be answered immediately by a God who
loves you." Or, "Just touch your television screen along with
praying, send in three easy payments by check or credit card,
and you will experience happy results." When prayers are not
answered as hoped, the TV religious salesman offers a sad,
guilt-filled response that implies, "You lacked faith," or "You

did not pray right," or "Perhaps you are being too selfish." We are left with a feeling that unanswered prayer is our own fault.

Both disappointment with God and disillusionment with His messengers are often cited by those who have rejected faith and no longer believe in prayer. Who can blame them?

The list is long of distinguished thinkers who have reached the unmistakable conclusion that bad things do happen to good people, and even godly people are capable of ungodly actions. Believing in God will not protect us against experiencing stress, grief, and disappointment. Prayers are not always answered immediately with positive results.

In his book *When Bad Things Happen to Good People*, Rabbi Harold Kushner argues that human suffering is a part of life's design. He suggests that the world has been created with love as God's central value. By definition, love cannot be forced. It takes at least two parties to enter freely into a loving relationship. A world that includes freedom as necessary to make love possible also allows the opposite to happen. Sometimes people choose not to love. If freedom is necessary as a vital ingredient in love, then randomness also must be included in life's design. Consequently, bad things can happen because of our intentional decisions or by random accident. Kushner's beliefs about bad things happening grew out of him wrestling with the tragedy of his son dying at a young age from a rare disease with no known cure. The death of his son was contrary to all of his prayers.

Philip Yancey, in his book *Where is God When It Hurts?*, adds to the discussion of human suffering by sharing a helpful insight offered by Dr. Paul Brand, a physician in a leper colony. Brand observed that the design of our nervous system, responsible for delivery of pain messages, actually serves healthy persons as an important line of defense that can protect us against further harm. Because we can feel pain, we pull our hand back from an open flame and protect ourselves against more serious injury. Our pain, in other words, can be perceived as a gift.

Prayers are not always answered as we would choose. It is also true that dreadful things sometimes happen to good people. In the face of senseless suffering, no good answer exists that will satisfy a broken heart.

There are many persons whose life circumstances give them what seems to be good cause for not believing. Religious salesmen with simplistic ideas about prayer have nothing helpful to say to survivors of the Holocaust, those who live with disfigurement and profound handicaps, victims of crime, families whose loved ones were killed by a drunken driver, refugees who must endure the squalor of refugee camps, cancer patients, persons afflicted by Lou Gehrig's disease, or a mother forced to bury an infant who has died of hunger. Reasonable people can agree that prayers do not always deliver the answers we seek. Remarkably, however, there are many who live with the above conditions and who have grown to lead lives of deeper belief in God. Why is it that some people can be crushed by pain and react negatively at the very mention of God, while others can experience the same terrible circumstances and draw upon faith in a life-giving way?

M. Scott Peck, in his popular book, *The Road Less Traveled*, observed that while we are right to acknowledge the bad things that happen to good people, we should also know that many bad things are prevented because of human goodness. That is, the same random chance that contributes to suffering also can lead to a fortunate circumstance that believers call a God incident.

Take a closer look at prayer. How is it possible to experience disappointment and still believe in God? Some approach prayer with the idea that God invites us to sit on His lap and turn in our wish list, much like a spiritual Santa Claus. There are scripture passages in the Gospels which might lead us to think of prayer in this way. In Matthew 21 Jesus teaches His disciples: "Whatever you ask in prayer, you will receive, if you have faith." There is ample evidence that sometimes prayers are answered in this remarkable "ask and you shall receive" fashion. But it is a shallow view of prayer if we live convinced that God exists only to give us what we want when we want it. It is wrong to assume that prayer's only purpose is to satisfy our immediate wants.

Those who pray will testify that often when we pray, the prayed-for results are not evident at all. Yet sometimes we pray and the presence of the Almighty feels close, like that of a good friend standing nearby to offer assurance. On other occasions, prayers can be offered and it feels like no one is listening. Prayer is not married to feelings. Prayer is not mainly about feeling warm and fuzzy, nor is prayer mainly about getting our way. Our relationship with God does not rest on our feelings which can burn hot or cold over time, nor is our relationship with God dependent on our awareness of God's activity. God is far more than an impersonal vending machine dispensing miracles according to our expressed desires. Prayer is given a firm foundation in a personal relationship with God. Prayer involves a personal decision to believe in God. Prayer is an act of faith. The Bible promises to believers that faith will be rewarded with God's forgiveness, God's guidance, God's eternal promise, God's presence, and God's purpose.

Prayer, at its best, is a means for growing a relationship with God. It is a method for sharing with God our public hopes and our private fears. We can come to God with our anger and our guilt. We can use prayer to thank God for blessings and to seek divine help and guidance in time of trial. Prayer is a reminder that we need not face life alone. Prayer is also one of the habits of faithful living that, as it is practiced, works over time to shape us as Christians. Those who make prayer a regular part of their daily routine often remark that prayer is an activity where God's direction for their living becomes clearer. Prayer creates opportunity for God incidents to happen.

Author and teacher Dr. John Savage has observed that each person is much like an iceberg. The tip of every iceberg can be seen, but most of the iceberg is hidden beneath the waves of the ocean. The part of the ice that is hidden is very large and continuously growing. We add to this under water private part of our existence as life happens around us. Our dog dies. Our friend moves away. Our boss changes at work. Our children get injured at a sporting event. Eventually life can get too heavy, and we let out a cry for help. Most often the cry for help is indirect, and sometimes it is even unhealthy. Addiction, depression, and acts of violence can be expressions of a hurting soul struggling for help. When life gets too heavy, what many of us really need is to believe that we are heard. We need to know in our pain we are still loved, our grief is a normal response to life's difficulty, and we are not alone. Prayer can be a lifeline to God's help with the challenges of life.

It is no accident that prayer is a central component of the world's many faiths. Judaism, Christianity, Islam, Hinduism, and Buddhism all feature prayer as an important spiritual practice. The Bible names religious leaders from the first chapters through the last who engaged God in conversational prayer as a means of understanding life and aiming to do God's will.

Early in my ministry, and with a desire to learn more about healing prayer, I attended a weekend retreat, led by a well-known healer who had several books and a large following to his credit. I was impressed. He was clearly a devout practitioner of healing prayer and was well-educated in medical science. I was impressed also by his complete honesty about his own experience. He did not know how prayer worked for healing, nor could he explain why healing prayer sometimes did not work, but he prayed for others as a servant of God. My roommate at the retreat was a Roman Catholic missionary priest from Central America who had come to the United States for surgery on a disintegrated disc which had left him in constant pain and without much mobility. At the conclusion of the retreat, he offered himself for healing prayer. He was healed. In a matter of minutes his disc mended itself and transformed the lives of all who witnessed it. His miracle transformed his ministry and energized the conference. The event was a God incident that cemented for me belief in the power and goodness of God. I was enthused by this experience of healing prayer.

Following the retreat, I returned to my employment as an on-call chaplain at the emergency room of a major metropolitan hospital. During my first night back, I was summoned to be with a family that included a wife and three young children. The father/husband, in his early 30s, had just experienced a major heart attack while driving his family to a long-awaited summer vacation. Inspired by my still-fresh experience with the healing power of prayer, I gathered the family together in a circle, and we prayed mightily together for the healing of their father/husband. We all felt the spiritual power of that moment. The conclusion of our heartfelt prayer was followed almost immediately by an ashen-faced physician who came into the waiting room and mumbled, "I'm sorry; he's gone. We did everything we could, and there was nothing more we could do."

I felt mugged by God. Anger surged in me. I grieved with the family whose world had been shattered. I wanted to quit ministry. I could not understand a God Who would answer prayer in such dramatic fashion on one occasion and then totally ignore legitimate group pleas the next day.

A mentor heard my pain and recommended a spiritual retreat. The spiritual director invited me to express my pain to God in a letter. He informed me after reading my 17-page, single-spaced writing that God had heard my pain, accepted my anger, and loved even this part of me.

I left that retreat knowing pain is real. Grief is a normal response to life's difficult circumstances. Death happens to us all. Sometimes prayers are not answered as we hope. Bad things do happen to good people. God is much larger than making life turn out for me as I want it when I want it. It is also true God is present in the miracles of answered prayer. I still pray for miracles regularly, but God also can be present in the questions and the passion of our painful disappointments. I have felt real anger and loss. In time I found relief in the permission given me to share my unvarnished feelings in an atmosphere of loving acceptance.

When faced with real-life disappointment, we can respond in many ways, including rejecting God, believing in God but staying angry, readjusting belief about prayer to accommodate the new reality, and/or trusting that in time God will answer prayer in ways we never expected. Many choose to continue to believe in God no matter what the circumstance because prayer has deepened a meaningful relationship with God. They continue to believe because they know God is with them as they walk through the valley of the shadow of death. They know it is especially when life's circumstances are most dark that we need the hope faith can offer. Others continue to believe in God because they know authentic faith produces better consequences for our living than does disbelief. Still others hold fast to prayer upheld by past memories of God which continue to give them hope even when God seems absent.

CHAPTER 20

GOD INCIDENTS

CAN YOU SEE

THE HAND OF GOD?

I WOULD NOT have thought about writing a book on God incidents were it not for Fred. God worked through Fred to make me more aware of God's presence in life, and I thank Fred for opening my eyes. This story may do the same for you.

I met Fred in the spring of 1986. I had preached my first sermon at a church where I had been appointed as an emergency replacement for a pastor who had been forced into early retirement. Any happiness I felt over receiving a new assignment that at first felt like a promotion soon vanished. After my introductory meeting, the chairman of the church board said: "Pastor, the finances are in the dumps, the boiler for the church doesn't work, we have a secretary who can't type, the roof leaks and needs to be replaced, the town is suffering economically, and our former pastor was carried from the church on a stretcher after the last church finance meeting. When the bishop asked us what we were looking for in a new pastor, we said: 'Bishop, we don't care who you send to us. You can send to us a slab of raw meat. Just make sure that raw meat has a chance for survival here.'"

Shortly after arriving, I was approached by a member of the local veteran's group. He asked: "As the new pastor, would you be willing to give the invocation and the annual message at the Veteran's Memorial following the Memorial Day parade?" Grateful for the sacrifices made by our troops, I gladly accepted the invitation.

Following an impressive parade to the cemetery and opening remarks by dignitaries, it was time for the new pastor to deliver the address. I stepped to the microphone. Before a word left my lips, lightning shot across the suddenly darkened sky followed by a thunderous clap, a strong breeze, and torrential rain. The gathered crowd immediately deserted the memorial for their cars. A faithful remnant ran for the cover of large trees in the old part of the cemetery 30 yards away.

The memory of war stories and the valor of our veterans at places like Bunker Hill, Normandy, and Iwo Jima kept me at the microphone, delivering my message honoring those who offered the ultimate sacrifice. Driving rain on a bald head is a cold distraction, but I slogged on.

The following Sunday, Fred introduced himself in the receiving line after the service. One of the congregation's veterans, Fred had been present at the parade and the cemetery ceremony. He came to church to thank me for my part, and then handed me a gift in appreciation. He said, "Here, I think you could use this." Fred's present was a blue baseball cap with gold lettering across the front. The message read, "God made a few perfect heads. The rest He gave hair."

I noticed that Fred's 80-year-old face was lined with laugh lines and wisdom wrinkles. He wore casual clothes. Fred had gentle blue eyes, big hands leathery from years of manual labor, and white wispy hair around a head that was as bald as mine. He enjoyed life as a permanent bachelor.

On another Sunday after church, Fred approached me at the back of the sanctuary, where we stood between buckets catching steady drips of a recent rain. He was the last person out of church that morning. "Pastor, I understand that you'd like some help paying for a new roof for the church."

"That's right, Fred," I said.

"Well, pastor, I have a gift to give you that I think will help pay for the roof."

"That's great. I am always open to receiving gifts, particularly when it is for a good cause like the church roof."

"Pastor, my only hesitation is that my sister said I shouldn't give you this gift and that you wouldn't want it."

"Fred, don't listen to your sister. Of course I am willing to receive your gift."

"Are you sure? She didn't think this was a good idea."

"Fred, I'm positive. What is the gift?"

Fred replied with enthusiasm: "I want to give you my slot machine."

I gasped, realizing that I had stepped in it this time. That week, our bishop had been quoted on the front page of the Chicago Tribune for his outspoken opposition to casino gambling. He had sent out an appeal for every pastor to be involved in the war against gambling.

"A slot machine?" I repeated. "Fred, even though we would probably pay off our roofing needs in no time if we set up a slot machine in the men's room, I'm pretty sure that the church wouldn't go for it."

"No, no. You don't understand. I don't want you to set the slot machine up in the church. I want you to sell it You see, I have a rare slot machine. It's an antique, a 1901 Mills-Dewey two-bit slot machine in mint condition. I think it's worth some money. You can sell the machine and then apply the funds to the church to help pay for the new roof."

I replied: "Oh, that sounds interesting. At the moment I don't know anything about slot machines, but I do know that we cannot keep the machine at the church. How about if you keep your gift at your house, and then, if I can figure something out, I'll let you know?"

Fred said: "That's OK by me."

On Tuesday, I officiated at a funeral and missed the luncheon meeting of the Rotary Club. Rotary stressed perfect attendance and fined members if they missed a meeting and did not make up their attendance at another club in the same week.

I decided to make up my missed meeting later in the week at the Rotary Club in a neighboring community. After lunch and during the club announcement time, a member of that club who was seated at the same table with me stood up to speak. I gathered from his announcement that he was the owner and director of a nearby antique museum. After his announcement, out of curiosity I asked, "Do you know anything at all about antique slot machines?"

His eyes lit up like a kid in a candy store, "Do I know anything about antique slot machines? It just so happens that I'm the largest dealer of these in the entire state of Illinois."

"Well, if I owned a 1901 antique Mills-Dewey two-bit slot machine in mint condition and wanted to sell it, how would I go about it?"

"You have one of those!? And you're a pastor!? Where did you get it?"

"Well, for the sake of discussion, if I did have one, how would I sell it?"

"There's only one place to sell that machine if you want to get what it is worth. You need to sell it at the world's largest slot-machine show."

My interest was quickened.

"When and where is that held?"

"It's tomorrow. And it is held at a resort about 32 miles from here."

Have you ever had the sense that God was talking and trying to get a message to you? This was one of those moments for me.

"And if I wanted to sell this machine at the slot machine show, how would I do that?"

"You have to become a dealer."

I felt myself getting in deeper.

"How do I become a dealer?" I asked, while thinking, "The bishop is really not going to like this."

The museum director said, "You are a pastor, and this is for a church, right?"

I nodded.

He said: "Let me make you an offer. I'm going to your town right after this meeting to pick up something else for my antique museum. I would be happy to swing by and take a look at your slot machine. I will tell you, in my best judgment, what I think it is worth. I will pick up the machine in my truck and take it to the slot-machine show and display it in my booth, which is the first one inside the front door. I will try to sell your machine for you. If I get an offer, I will call you up, and you can decide if you would like to sell it. Then I will close the deal and bring you the money, and I won't charge you anything for doing this. Is that OK with you?"

All I could say was: "Thank you, Jesus."

He did what he promised. He estimated the value of the slot machine at $6,500.

Friday morning I got a call from the slot machine show. It was my new friend who said: "Pastor, somebody must be looking out for you because this has never happened to me before. I pulled up my truck at the convention center to unload it, opened the back door, and while I was climbing into the truck, a man walked by, saw your machine, and offered me $9,500 cash for it on the spot. He is standing here with me waiting for your answer. What should I do?"

I said, "Sell."

That night I made a cash deposit at the bank for the church of $9,500. Never in the 100-year history of that church had anyone made a $9,500 Friday night cash deposit.

On Saturday, I went into the bank to take care of the rest of the paper work. I introduced myself, saying I was the pastor and had made a night deposit the previous evening. The teller said: "Oh, we know who you are. What kind of bingo game are you running up at that church anyway?"

I tell this story, not because of the slot machine or the miracle of its sale, or because Fred's gift inspired the people of the church to raise enough to cover the cost of replacing the roof, but because of what Fred shared with me when I told him about the sale.

He said: "Pastor, I have to tell you why I gave you that slot machine. In World War II, I enlisted with my very best friend from town. We went through basic training and were shipped out together. We were in the same unit, a couple of privates. We saw action on the islands of the Pacific. One day there was a Japanese bombing run on our position. My buddy and I were in the same foxhole; the bomb went off nearby, and the foxhole collapsed around us. A couple of hours later when we were dug out, they pulled my best friend's body off of me. He died and bled over me, and if he had not taken the shrapnel, it would have killed me.

"Every single day since then I have lived with the unforgettable memory that every breath I have taken is a gift bought with a price, and that the person who loved me most died so that I might have life. I'd work my factory job and come home and listen to my records and sing my songs. I bought the slot machine years ago from the VFW for $15 when it became illegal to have them operating in public establishments. Ever since then, that slot machine has sat in my room like some kind of idol. I polished it, and took care of it, but I just knew I had to give it to the church because, when I finally get to heaven and look my buddy in the eye, I want to be able to tell him, 'Thanks. You didn't die in vain.'"

This experience with Fred and his 1901 Mills-Dewey two-bit slot machine in mint condition opened my eyes to God incidents. I am convinced that Fred's offer, and the subsequent events which led to the sale of that slot machine, were not merely coincidence or accidents of chance. Rather they revealed the fingerprints of God in order to inspire greater faith.

What I heard from Fred that day was not just a God incident. Fred shared with me the gospel, and some of the deepest insight I ever have received. There is someone Who loves us best, Who has died that we might have life and the promise of eternity. The lesson from that God incident has inspired my purpose for living: Life is best lived as a thank-you note for the greater love that has been offered up for us by God.

Life here on earth is a fleeting gift. We never know when we, too, will be called home. There is no time like the present to live with eternity in mind, so when we get to heaven and see our Lord face to face, we can honestly and profoundly thank Him with words I heard from Fred: "Lord, I want You to know You did not die in vain."

CHAPTER 21

INCIDENTS

FOR

COMMUNITY

CAN GOD BE experienced by an entire community?

God incidents can be personal. Individuals meet God in a God incident and are inspired to greater faithfulness or to find a faith in the first place. Yet, it is also true that faith in God is experienced not just when we are alone. Faith is intended to be a shared experience as a part of a larger community of believers. In 1 Corinthians 12 the Apostle Paul describes how following Jesus is like being part of a human body. Each of us is necessary. Teamwork is required. Christ is our head.

The gifts of God, like a buffet line at a wedding feast, are intended for all the guests at the event. God incidents can also be experienced by a multitude. Jews, Christians, and Muslims all recognize the giving of the Ten Commandments to Moses as a God incident. The commands are intended both for individuals and for the benefit of the whole community. These laws helped a large group of people survive in their journey from slavery to freedom in one of the world's most difficult environments. Without the willingness of the Israelite people to promise to obey the commandments of God, powerful enemies, human anarchy, or the desperate needs for survival could have torn the group apart.

Another well-known community God incident is found in the New Testament – the story of Jesus feeding 5,000 on the shores of the Sea of Galilee. All four of the New Testament gospels remember this dramatic event. In John, the generosity of a child is highlighted. Jesus used a child's gift of five loaves and two fish to feed the crowd. When all had been satisfied, there were 12 baskets of leftovers, an object lesson about God's generosity for the reluctant disciples that has motivated concern for the collective good ever since.

This God incident also teaches that God is often made known, not merely to individuals, but to whole groups of people. We each can experience the life-shaping power of a God incident when we are engaged with others in doing great good for God.

It is not unusual for teams of people engaged in projects for the common good – such as conducting a community food drive to feed the hungry, working with relief organizations to help devastated communities rebuild, or rallying neighbors to raise funds for an important need – to experience the presence, power, and inspiration of God through the combined effort.

For example, Brent helped an entire town experience a God incident. When Brent was a year and a half old, he was diagnosed with leukemia that was affecting 80 percent of his body. He was put on an immediate regimen of chemotherapy, and his little body responded in textbook fashion. By necessity, his mother, Sarah, immersed herself in nursing duties, and took a crash course about leukemia and the demanding requirements of treatment. Brent received spinal taps every month for two and a half years to monitor his condition, though doctors pronounced Brent to be a low-risk patient with an 80-90 percent chance of recovery. When given the hope that Brent had the "best kind of leukemia for recovery," Sarah was reassured. No one realized how that promise would be tested in the days ahead.

Near to Brent's second birthday, his parents presented their son for baptism. Members of the congregation affirmed their part in the baptismal covenant with these words:

"With God's help, we will so order our lives after the example of Christ that Brent will be surrounded with steadfast love and confirmed and strengthened in the way that leads to life eternal."[21]

When Brent was 4, after a brief period of remission, the leukemia returned with a vengeance. Brent was readmitted to the hospital for renewed heavy doses of chemotherapy that put him back into critical care. For Brent to survive his relapse he would need a bone-marrow transplant. Brent's mom was exhausted. She called her pastor and asked for congregational assistance in trying to find a donor. She could not give Brent both the care he needed to survive and also conduct the massive fundraising and donor-search campaigns needed to save Brent's life. The first problem was out of three and a half million people on the National Bone Marrow Donor Registry, the few possible matches for Brent had already been ruled incompatible. A second problem was money: the $65 cost to screen each person, the cost to add their blood typing information to the national registry, and the possible $250,000 cost of a transplant were staggering sums for a family already burdened with medical bills.

Few thought that Brent's church would be able to register more than 50 new marrow donor volunteers for the cause. But that baptism promise kept echoing in the congregation's collective consciousness. The church family had no choice but to proceed.

In the biblical story of the feeding of the 5,000, Jesus took the simple offering of a single boy and turned it into a feast for a multitude. In this contemporary story, God took a simple first step from a cautious pastor and a supportive church

---

21 *The Book of Hymns,* The United Methodist Publishing House, Nashville, Tennessee, 1966, #828

for a child with leukemia and thereby revealed great glory. Volunteers were needed. Brent's pastor extended a general plea for help and hoped for three or four to attend a brainstorming session to explore how the church might help. Surprisingly, 40 volunteers showed up and immediately began organizing fundraisers. It seemed doubtful that the fundraisers would bring in more than a few thousand dollars. But God was in charge. Volunteers looked beyond the obstacles and focused instead on their love for Brent. Herculean tasks were undertaken by volunteers, such as a garage sale – executed from collection, to pricing, to sale, to close down in just three days – which netted close to $10,000.

People engaged in fundraising on their feet and in prayer on their knees. Money began pouring in – first in hundreds, then in thousands, and finally like a tidal wave. A church from a distant city heard about Brent and sent a check for $20,000; a prison inmate who heard about Brent sent permission to use his blood if he proved a match; a worker at a local factory brought in a jug of cash from her department; grandmothers organized to raise funds from gas stations. The funds raised far exceeded expectations. Brent's tiny community raised more than $100,000 for a child most did not even know. Ordinary citizens did extraordinary things for Brent. Even better, strangers who were neighbors became friends in the unifying cause to give Brent a chance. Those who worked on his cause discovered they were part of a "can-do" community with a huge heart!

Brent re-entered the hospital as a full-time patient. No one could foresee he would spend seven of the next eight months there. He was the first patient ever to live in the special hermetically-sealed hospital room at the regional children's hospital.

During the community's annual summer civic celebration, God worked a miracle in Brent's hometown when 1,200 people stood in line at the local community center. Most paid $65 apiece for the privilege of having their blood tested to be added to the National Bone Marrow Donor Registry for Brent. An hour after the daylong blood drive was supposed to be over, donors still made a line around the room and out the door, patiently waiting their turn in the Saturday heat for the chance to save a child's life. While the drive was taking place, others were praying for Brent at his nearby church.

The unprecedented donor drive made headlines across Brent's home state and was followed by other drives on his behalf in other cities. A nearby university blood program and the local chapter of the American Red Cross both donated their assistance. Many local celebrities took turns in a dunk tank to raise hope and needed cash for Brent. Publicity around the donor drive raised local, regional, and national awareness to the need for marrow donors.

As Brent's condition grew more critical, important decisions had to be made. The regional children's hospital announced the hiring of a pediatric bone marrow and leukemia specialist, and the opening of a pediatric marrow transplant program. The search of the national registry turned up empty for Brent, but the local marrow drive began identifying matches immediately for others needing transplants.

When it seemed Brent had run out of options, a single frozen umbilical cord from Milan, Italy, was found which matched perfectly all six antigens of his blood. The cord was flown to Brent's hospital and thawed. The person who analyzed the blood for a match said: "If I did not know better, this match is so perfect that it could have been Brent's own umbilical cord." With cord blood, unlike a marrow transplant from a living human donor, the transplant of life giving T-cells has only one chance to succeed. Brent received massive doses of radiation at the hospital every day for a week prior to the transplant. He rode his tricycle down from his room through the hospital to receive the near-deadly radiation.

In October of that year, Brent made history as the first child at the regional children's hospital to receive a pediatric cord-blood transplant. On a night when President Bill Clinton, Yasser Arafat, King Hussein, and Benjamin Netanyahu signed an historic peace accord in the Middle East, Brent was the lead story on the region's evening news. Brent's family flew an Italian flag at their home in gratitude.

Brent's community held its collective breath and spent much time in prayer. Phone calls to the boy's church regularly began with, "How's Brent?" A pastor from a nearby city called to ask about Brent, then added, "We've been praying for him every day in our 5:00 a.m. prayer group." Each day was a gift for a child who would have died without the transplant.

When Brent finally came home from the hospital, there was rejoicing in the community which had raised funds, secured donors, and spent time in prayer on his behalf. Brent again was the lead story in the evening news. But reality never left his home. His parents were overwhelmed by the needs. Brent still required weekly clinic visits, regular spinal taps, tube feeding, regular dressing changes, and endless cycles of medication. He had to learn again skills of a 4-year-old boy. He could not eat on his own and had to relearn how to sleep. Every day required physical and occupational therapy.

Brent moved very slowly and required constant care, but he was making steady progress toward recovery. He talked with hope about the day his feeding tube could be removed from his stomach. He was starting to enjoy life. That spring he went to his kindergarten roundup with 50 classmates to get a taste of what school would be like in the fall.

As the sample kindergarten class began, Sarah was fearful for her fragile child. But Brent was bigger than mom's worry: He was the happiest child there. When the other children were asked to come to the front of the room and sit down and cross their legs, Brent struggled to walk and tried to lower himself to the floor, in obvious discomfort, unable to cross his legs. Brent was proud that he got to pick out his own seat on the bus and was excited to begin kindergarten in the fall.

Sarah asked: "Brent, do you think we should work on crossing your legs, so that you'll know how to do this when school starts?"

Brent responded: "No, mom, we don't have any homework in kindergarten."

Sarah asked Brent how the rest of his day went. "I was a little nervous," he said, "but I was having so much fun, I forgot about it."

In early May, Brent made one of his two monthly visits to the clinic. The test results were not good. A blood test revealed that Brent's leukemia had returned. There were no more medical answers. On the darkest day of his parents' lives, the evening sky was colored by the most magnificent rainbow Brent's parents had ever seen. This biblical symbol of hope infused them with strength to continue.

Two weeks later, Brent's parents returned to the clinic. The doctor told them what lay ahead and what to expect. He urged them to do a lifetime of parenting in a very little time. A call was made to the "Make a Wish Foundation," and in 24 hours Brent and his parents were being driven to the airport in a limousine for a trip to Disney World.

When he returned home, Brent wanted to play until after dark. He rode a new three-wheeler around the yard and through a river his parents made, splashing mud and water on his Dad's toes. Brent was fixed up so he could drive with his morphine pump attached to the handle bars to help keep his pain under control.

Hospice was called as Brent's condition rapidly worsened. On his final day, Brent raised his arms straight up toward the ceiling as if reaching for someone and called out: "Hold my hand."

Sarah reached to hold her son's hand, and Brent pushed her away and said, "Not you," as if to tell his Mom someone else was there to take his hand. Brent died shortly after.

Brent's life was a God incident. Through this child God impacted not just one person, but was revealed in the efforts of many. Brent's battle with a disease that took his life awakened a community to the power of compassion. Because of Brent, 1,200 people were added to the National Bone Marrow Donor Registry; an endowment for ministry to needy children was established; 13 persons received lifesaving bone marrow transplants; a cord-blood bank was established at a state university; and a pediatric marrow transplant program was established at a regional children's hospital.

In the week following Brent's death, an unusual event happened. Linda, identified as a match for someone else after Brent's bone marrow drive, was summoned to the hospital as a donor for another leukemia patient. Her pastor traveled to the hospital to be a supportive presence. Shortly before the scheduled procedure, Linda was visited by the physician who was to perform the operation. It was Brent's doctor. For a few moments the doctor did not recognize the pastor or the donor. He asked Linda: "How did you happen to become a bone-marrow donor here today."

She replied: "Brent."

The three pairs of eyes in that hospital room locked into a moment of holy recognition. A donor, a pastor, and a doctor were all aware they were participants in a much larger and more important movement of God's Holy Spirit. Through the life of one small child, God had been made known in a God incident which was not just a single moment of glory touching an individual. Like the flight of a comet through the night sky, God moved through a divine path that still causes many who remember Brent to give thanks.

Our ability to discern the movement of God may depend on our perspective. Grief over Brent's death prompted some to turn away from God, angry that prayers for his survival were disappointed. Sadly, Brent's parents divorced after their son's death due to insurmountable and irreconcilable issues compounded by his death. Brent's story points out two truths about life which exist in tension: God is present, and so is pain.

Brent's story, like many others, helps us remember God incidents are meant not just to help strengthen the faith of individuals. God incidents are a seed for growing community.

CHAPTER 22

GODINCIDENTS

IN

HUMAN FORM

HAVE YOU EVER met someone who has inspired you to become a better person?

Christians believe what Jesus teaches in John 14. If we love God and keep God's commandments, then through the power of the Holy Spirit God will take up spiritual residence inside us. The Apostle Paul reinforced this idea that our lives are hosts for the presence of God when he wrote: "Do you not know that your body is a temple of the Holy Spirit within you, which you have from God? You are not your own; you were bought with a price. So glorify God with your bodies." (1 Corinthians 6:19-20)

It should be no surprise, then, that one of the most common places for us to experience a God incident is in relationship with others. There are ordinary human beings who have learned to combine a living faith with a steady practice of loving others. People who meet them are regularly moved to live with greater faithfulness themselves. We are all capable of choosing to make a difference where we live.

Bill and Bobbie have been disciples who have helped me to see God more clearly. They are modest folk who retired and found a calling late in life as the managers of an inner-city soup kitchen. Five nights a week, for many years, between five and seven hours per shift, Bill and Bobbie managed the preparation and serving of a free evening meal in a gracious setting to 125 persons. Most of those receiving this hospitality are poor. The food and fellowship are highlights in their day and an important lifeline for their living.

Over 30 churches partner to support the soup kitchen, but it was Bill and Bobbie whose day-in and day-out faithfulness made it happen. Being around this busy couple was a humbling experience. They were clear that loving and serving Christ by feeding the hungry was their motivation. During a season of life when many other adults are thinking about dropping out of active engagements, this retired couple practiced discipleship. Their commitment inspired many others to give of themselves sacrificially for the same cause and awakened deep admiration in me that said: "Lord, please help me to grow like this couple in devotion to you."

Susan is another of God's special people. After retiring from a career as a schoolteacher, she decided helping poor children learn to read by pairing them with an adult mentor for an hour each week was the greatest gift she could give back to her community. Susan partnered with her church and an inner-city elementary school with a goal that each child would be reading at grade level by the time they graduated. Today, 150 volunteers are helping Susan's vision become a reality. Susan's witness is not flashy. She is not interested in accolades or rewards. Many in her community will give this woman's name when citing reasons for their own faith. Susan inspired me to think about volunteering an hour a week for a year in an elementary school near where I lived, and the relationship I established with a fifth-grader helped a child learn to read and filled me with a sense of great satisfaction.

The late Mother Teresa is another of God's humble workers. She was awarded the Nobel Peace Prize in 1979 for her global work devoted to caring for the needs of the poorest of the poor. In 1982, she heard of a house in Lebanon where special needs children were trapped in the middle of a killing zone between enemies. The soldiers on both sides had refused to cease fire to allow the innocents to be evacuated. Mother Teresa, moved by the situation, had sisters in her order pray through the night. She flew to Lebanon. When the combatants learned Mother Teresa had come, they stopped their shooting long enough to enable her to evacuate the children. Persons like her are so faithful that there is a spiritual presence about them which helps others to see God and do God's will.

We all know persons who help us see God more clearly: Diane, who has devoted herself to bringing education to a community in Latin America; John, who spends his vacations drilling wells in Africa so villages can have clean water; or women quilters who labor for no publicity to make quilts for veterans. And there are many others.

The world is full of ordinary people who help make God known through their own faithful witness. They minister to the dying in hospice, they tutor children in the inner city, they run Bible studies in prisons, they organize health clinics among the poorest villages of the world, and they volunteer in nursing homes. I am inspired by friends who choose to risk themselves in hotspots around the world, giving witness to the importance of peace with justice. Through their efforts, others are inspired to offer themselves in similar gestures of devotion to God. A great way to get to know God is to pattern our life after the inspirational example of those all around us who help us see God's love more clearly.

The words of a beloved hymn by Lesbia Scott say it well:

> *I sing a song of the saints of God,*
> *patient and brave and true,*
> *who toiled and fought and lived and died*
> *for the Lord they loved and knew.*
>
> *The world is bright with the joyous saints*
> *who love to do Jesus' will.*

*You can meet them in school, on the street, in the
store,
in church, by the sea, in the house next door;
they are saints of God, whether rich or poor,
and I mean to be one, too.*[22]

Seek to know God more fully and to make God known.
Experience your life as the God incident it is, and use God's
love to make a difference. Be more aware of the next time God
is made known to you in an incident of Holy presence. When
that incident occurs, ask yourself this important question:
"Lord, what can I learn from this?" May your questions lead
you to a deeper relationship with God.

---

22 From, "I Sing a Song of the Saints of God" by Lesbia Scott, 1929.

Discussion Questions

Chapter 1

1. Do you believe in God? Why or why not?
2. Do you know persons who have an adverse reaction when faith is discussed?
3. Have you ever experienced a sequence of events that seemed to be more than coincidence? What did that event teach you about God? About yourself?
4. What do you think about the idea that there is a God who is revealed in such a sequence?
5. What difference does it make whether a person believes in God or not?

Chapter 2

1. Do you agree that in God's math everybody counts? What evidence in life supports or refutes that idea?
2. Have you ever felt God's presence near you? Describe your experience.
3. Have you ever witnessed faithful people loving others in such a way that you were inspired to be good yourself?
4. Have you ever experienced a God incident like that described in the line from Natalie Sleeth's *Hymn of Promise*, "unrevealed until its season, something God alone can see"?
5. Some people experience hardship and shake their fist at God. For others, faith is strengthened through trial.

What contributes to these different responses? What are the consequences of each?

Chapter 3

1. What do you understand a miracle to be?
2. Have you ever experienced a miracle? What was this like?
3. What does the author suggest as reasons for miracles? Do you agree?
4. How do we deal with the reality that sometimes miracles happen and other times they do not?
5. Why can two people look at the same event, and one sees it as a miracle while the other does not? What do miracles teach us about God?

Chapter 4

1. Have you ever been surprised by God? Describe.
2. What do you think about the claims made in this chapter that God sometimes uses the unlikeliest persons to accomplish His purposes?
3. Do you think that Cyrus, the Ninevites, the Samaritan, and Earl would have recognized themselves as God's agents?
4. Do you think of yourself as being used to accomplish God's purpose?
5. The opening illustration about the blind men of Indostan implies no one has the whole truth. Religions, Christianity included, frequently make claims to have the whole truth about God. What do you think about this?

Chapter 5

1. Is it OK to be angry at God?

2. Do you agree that sometimes we are able to see God more clearly in the scenic turn-out of history than we can in the present moment?

3. What do you think of Leslie Weatherhead's idea that God can use the difficult circumstances of our lives for God's greater glory?

4. Looking back over your own life journey, can you identify God incidents when your life took a significant turn?

Chapter 6

1. Where have you experienced the awesomeness of creation?

2. Can you point to evidence of divine design which helps you believe in God?

3. Does belief or disbelief affect God's decisions?

4. Are there aspects of science which you feel are aligned with religion? Other aspects that are not? Why?

Chapter 7

1. What is the most significant issue you have ever wrestled with?

2. What important life lessons can be learned from such wrestling?

3. How has the experience of wrestling changed you?

4. What does Paul's experience of hardship as described in his letters to the Corinthians suggest about the "prosperity gospel," which implies if we love God and

are faithful we will be rewarded materially with good things?

5. Was the author's emergency room encounter with Mildred a coincidence or a God incident? What is the difference?

Chapter 8

1. What is a core value you would die to defend?

2. Some people believe in a "survival of the fittest" world. Where do you see evidence supporting this idea? What are the consequences of living with that conviction?

3. Have you ever been broken? What has the experience of brokenness taught you?

4. Do you think there are places where God may be at work which we are unable to see in the present?

5. When history looks back on your life, as we do on Biblical characters from a perspective of over 3,000 years, what would you like future people to remember about you?

Chapter 9

1. Do you think there are some identifiable behaviors that, if chosen, are more likely than others to bring us closer to God?

2. Are there also behaviors that, if chosen, are likely to distance us from God?

3. Are there circumstances so desperate that some people have no choice but to engage in businesses such as drugs, gambling, and the sex trade in order to make a living? Do we see these persons differently than those who pursue the good? Why or why not?

4. Do you know a person whose faith is so authentic that it shines through them? What is it about this person you find attractive?

5. If it is a goal of yours to grow closer to God in this lifetime, what do you need to do to achieve this?

Chapter 10

1. What turn-around stories in your experience have made an impression on you?

2. Do you think faith can make a dramatic difference in the content and direction of life?

3. Have you ever been lost? How did you find your way?

4. What makes a turn-around a God incident?

5. For every alcoholic like John whose life has been turned around there are others who are unable to do so. What is your recipe for a successful about-face in life?

Chapter 11

1. What are some of the neighborhoods mentioned in the New Testament where Jesus said he would be? Have you experienced Jesus in such neighborhoods too?

2. Have you ever been in a place where it felt to you that God was totally absent?

3. Have you ever been in a place where it felt to you that God was totally present?

4. What are the moments in life when people are most receptive to hearing about faith from a friend?

5. Is God present in life as we experience it? What difference does believing or disbelieving in this possibility make in how we choose to live?

Chapter 12

1. Do you know anyone with a handicapping condition? What life lessons have you learned from them?
2. Have you ever experienced heightened danger when you had to trust someone or something else for your safety? What did you learn from that experience?
3. Do you agree there are Biblical principles for living which can help us stay in touch with God when our vision is otherwise clouded? Why or why not?
4. If you had to choose one core value to follow in your life, what would it be and why?
5. Does it help you to know even Jesus faced challenging moments like we do?

Chapter 13

1. Whom do you admire for serving as a model of courage in the face of adversity?
2. Can you affirm God at work in the midst of pain and suffering?
3. Some persons reject God when they experience hardship, while for others the trial inspires deeper faith. Why is this so?
4. What doubts do you have about God?
5. If faith in God is an act of personal will, and this is a choice among many options, what difference does this faith choice make in a time of difficulty?

Chapter 14

1. Can you identify places where we feel God especially near?
2. What holy ground moments have you experienced?
3. What can we learn about God by visiting sacred places?
4. What is the value in setting apart certain spaces as holy? For you personally? For the human community?
5. Why do you think people invest time, treasure, and talent to build sacred sanctuaries for worship?

Chapter 15

1. When have you ever experienced conflict?
2. What lessons has conflict taught you?
3. What good has come as a result?
4. Do you believe God can work through conflict?
5. What are some causes of conflict? What does it take to resolve conflict?

Chapter 16

1. What important life lesson have you learned from someone else? In what context was it learned?
2. Do you believe people can be used as instruments for the delivery of God's message?
3. How do we know if a message and a messenger are really from God?
4. What are some ways God speaks to the world?
5. What kind of people do you believe and why?

Chapter 17

1. Have you ever been asked to do something you did not want to do?
2. What are your major life commitments? What are these costing you? What inspired you to make them?
3. What is the hardest commandment for you to obey? Why?
4. What are the consequences for the human community when people choose not to honor their promises?
5. When have you stood up in opposition to the majority?

Chapter 18

1. Do you agree dreams can be a way to learn important things about ourselves and God?
2. What dreams do you remember that are important to you?
3. What is the danger in making a claim that all dreams come from God?
4. Some larger dreams are important for the way they shape society. Can you think of some of these dreams? Why are they important?
5. How can we tell if a dream is a God incident?

Chapter 19

1. What are your earliest memories of prayer? How have you experienced God through prayer?
2. When have you experienced prayers answered? Unanswered?

3. What do you think about the author's thought that prayers are not about "getting what we want" as much as they are vehicles for growing a relationship with God?
4. Why do bad things sometimes happen to good people?
5. Why do some people choose to believe in God despite difficult circumstances?

Chapter 20

1. Have you had someone give you a sacrificial gift that has changed your life?
2. What is the greatest gift you have ever given or received?
3. Do you think Fred's gift of a slot machine was a "God incident?" If so, where can you see God's fingerprints in this story?
4. Is generosity an important virtue to practice? Why or why not?
5. Was it appropriate for the pastor to accept Fred's gift, especially when he said they couldn't keep it on the church premises?

Chapter 21

1. What is more important to you, the welfare of a group or the happiness of an individual?
2. Why? What does the Bible suggest?
3. Do you agree that Brent's life was a communal God incident? Why or why not?
4. Brent died. Do God incidents have to have happy endings?
5. What is the value of a communal God incident as compared to one which is only experienced by an individual?

6. What are the challenges of living in community? Why should we bother to deal with these challenges?

Chapter 22

1. Whom do you admire as a role model?

2. The Bible makes a claim in John 14 that God will take up residence in the lives of those who do God's will and keep God's commandments. Do you know anyone whose living example shows that this claim is true?

3. Epicurus, a Greek philosopher, said: "Let us eat, drink, and be merry, for tomorrow we die," and promoted life that maximized pleasure and minimized pain. He yearned for a lovely walled garden where he could block out the worries of the world and have fulfilling conversations with good friends. What might motivate you to leave the garden and engage the world with its problems?

4. Many persons who are resuscitated following a near-death experience describe a meeting, during their period of registered death, with a being of light who asks them: "What have you done with the gift I have given you?" These persons may return to life reluctantly but with a new resolve to make their lives count for God. How would you answer that question regarding the fruits of your life? What are you doing with the gift of your life?

5. Human beings are capable of great evil and heroic good. What qualities of goodness do you wish to grow? What can you do to help achieve that goal?

6. Is faith a matter of belief or of actions? Does one have a greater impact than the other?

COURSE

STUDY GROUP

GOD INCIDENTS

OUTLINES

Four weeks (Advent):
    Week 1 Intro and Chapter 1
    Week 2 Chapter 4
    Week 3 Chapter 5
    Week 4 Chapter 19

Five weeks:
    Week 1 Intro and Chapter 1
    Week 2 Chapter 4
    Week 3 Chapter 5
    Week 4 Chapter 9
    Week 5 Chapter 19

Six weeks
    Week 1 Intro and Chapter 1
    Week 2 Chapter 4
    Week 3 Chapter 5
    Week 4 Chapter 9
    Week 5 Chapter 19
    Week 6 Chapter 20

Seven weeks (Lent)
    Week 1 Intro and Chapter 1
    Week 2 Chapter 4
    Week 3 Chapter 5
    Week 4 Chapter 9
    Week 5 Chapter 19
    Week 6 Chapter 20
    Week 7 Chapter 21

Nine weeks
    Week 1 Intro and Chapter 1
    Week 2 Chapter 4
    Week 3 Chapter 5
    Week 4 Chapter 9
    Week 5 Chapter 14

Week 6 Chapter 15
Week 7 Chapter 19
Week 8 Chapter 20
Week 9 Chapter 21

Twelve weeks

Week 1 Intro and Chapter 1
Week 2 Chapter 4
Week 3 Chapter 5
Week 4 Chapter 9
Week 5 Chapter 11
Week 6 Chapter 12
Week 7 Chapter 13
Week 8 Chapter 14
Week 9 Chapter 15
Week 10 Chapter 19
Week 11 Chapter 20
Week 12 Chapter 21

Acknowledgements

I COULD NOT have completed this book without the supportive love of family and the patient encouragement of my wife, Nancy. This book is more readable thanks to the editorial advice of Jennie Weber, and the constructive feedback of the Thursday morning breakfast men's group at Holt United Methodist Church. I am also indebted to the editorial advice and encouragement given by Dr. Douglas Wingeier, Dr. Lawrence Burns, Dr. William Reynolds, the Rev. Gunnar Carlson, Clayton Hardiman, Susan Harrison-Wolffis, Don Dahlstrom, Bishop Deb Kiesey, and Bishop Sharon Rader. Thanks to Bill Bode and David Crumm for your valued publishing expertise. I love the cover art and graphics help rendered by my cousin Ann Rhodes Riebe. I am grateful for many who participated in focus groups and who shared stories of their own God incidents. Thanks also to the many persons and congregations mentioned and unnamed here who have helped me to see God more clearly, to love God more dearly, and, I pray, to follow God more nearly.

Endorsements

From the very first page, God Incidents made me think about my own life and faith. It made me feel, question, remember, re-examine and look within. I can think of no finer compliment to give to my friend, Glenn Wagner, pastor and author: This book is worth reading.

-- Susan Harrison-Wolffis, retired columnist for MLive

Dr. Wagner has written a personal, compelling account of God Incidents that have touched his life and deeply move the reader. Coming from the experience of a thoughtful, caring pastor, this book brings theology and spirituality together in a way that motivates us to stay open to the divine activity in the everyday. An inspiring read.

-- Dr. Doug Wingeier, emeritus professor of practical theology, Garrett-Evangelical Theological Seminary

Glenn Wagner's God Incidents could not be more timely. Growing numbers of Americans tell researchers they either don't believe God exists, or aren't sure. The inspiring biblical and contemporary stories in God Incidents, recounting God's action in the world past and present, offer a compelling, hopeful and welcome Christian response.

-- Gunnar Carlson, former newspaper editor and retired United Methodist pastor

God matters! At the deepest level human beings strive to experience and know Spirit beyond self. Wagner encourages and gives insights into how paying attention to God sightings along the way will enrich and strengthen life.

-- **Sharon Rader, retired United Methodist bishop**

Glenn Wagner's God Incidents articulates clearly, lovingly, and directly the basic teachings of Christianity and its author's lived experience of these teachings.

-- **Dr. William Reynolds – dean for the arts and humanities at Hope College**

There is a depth of conviction and purpose in Glenn Wagner's God Incidents that lets you know this is the work of a lifetime. At times, when pastors, scholars and theologians discuss God's presence in our lives, a coolly academic quality surfaces, as if they are reciting by rote the elements of a lesson learned. Not so for Wagner. His look at how God becomes manifest in human experience draws not only on his many years of work as a pastor but also on his travels as a questioning, longing human being. The conclusions he draws are carefully considered and deeply felt.

-- **Clayton Hardiman – retired newspaper columnist and religion editor**

In a time when so many are searching for evidence of God in the world and in their lives, Rev. Dr. Glenn Wagner's book, God Incidents, offers an inspiring glimpse into 'God moments' from his own personal experiences and the experiences of those he has served throughout his ministry. These 'God moments' help connect us to something greater than ourselves. They can inspire and change our lives.

-- Deb Kiesey, bishop for the Michigan Area of the United Methodist Church